Law Ess

PROPERTY LAW

To Katya, Katarina and Filip

Law Essentials

PROPERTY LAW

Duncan Spiers, M.A. (Oxon)

Advocate,
Lecturer in Law, Napier University

DUNDEE UNIVERSITY PRESS
2008

First published in Great Britain in 2008 by
Dundee University Press
University of Dundee
Dundee DD1 4HN

www.dup.dundee.ac.uk

ISBN 978-1-84586-056-1

No natural forests were destroyed to make this product;
Only farmed timber was used and replanted.

British Library Cataloguing-in-Publication Data
A catalogue record for this book is available on request from the British Library.

Typeset by Waverley Typesetters, Fakenham
Printed and bound by Bell & Bain Ltd, Glasgow

CONTENTS

TABLE OF CASES

TABLE OF STATUTES

ACKNOWLEDGMENTS

A number of my friends have helped me in the writing of this volume. I particularly owe a debt to Ken Dale-Risk, who assisted in the writing of sections of Chapters 1 and 4 and who, with my other colleagues, Douglas Maule, Nicholas Grier and Alan Reid, read over the draft chapters and helped me to remove errors of content, style and typography. I would like to thank them all and hope that the result is worthy of all their efforts.

1 INTRODUCTION AND GENERAL CONCEPTS

INTRODUCTION

Property law in Scotland is a large and complex but important area of law, governing all manner of rights and obligations concerning land and other types of possessions. It is large because of the wide range of different types of property which can be held. It is complex because of the range of different rights and obligations which can arise in these types of property. It is quite possible for a number of people to hold different interests in one item of property at one and the same time. It is for this reason that it is sometimes said that property involves a "bundle of rights". Property law is important because our possessions have enormous economic value and significance. Indeed, it is impossible to envisage any form of economy without property. Economic values are a particular type of values acknowledged by civilised societies and this social aspect of property law is of considerable significance since, in some instances, items of property may have no physical existence at all. Such items are referred to in the law as "incorporeal property" and involve things as disparate as shares in a company, rights to copyright in a created work or rights to a trade mark. Property law needs to have the ability to address all of these types of economic and social values as well as applying to more mundane physical items such as goods, money and land. The various ways in which people can take possession of different types of property, retain control over them, transfer them or recover possession of them when dispossessed of them involves an understanding of the various types of property classification recognised by the law.

Not surprisingly, the principles of Scots law have ancient foundations. To a great extent these are derived from the Roman law, which was imported into Scots law at the height of the Renaissance and modified and laid down by the Institutional Writers, notably Bankton, Stair, Erskine and Bell in their various *Institutions* of the laws of Scotland. But this Roman law system was overlaid on an existing system of law, which in the case of land law involved overlaying the carefully analytical and coherent Roman law principles over a somewhat legally coarse feudal system. The resultant effect was a hybrid system of land law with some of the attributes of both sources but, as time progressed, Scots land law more than proved itself capable of development to accommodate the effect (on property law) of both the growth in urban population and the industrial growth of the 19th century. The influence of feudal law has, however, been significantly lessened by the Abolition of Feudal Tenure etc (Scotland) Act 2000.

There will be no attempt to lay out the principles of the historical Roman law in this volume, however, the interested reader can examine Book II ("Of Things") of Justinian's *Institutes* which is readily available on the Internet. There, the reader will find the treatment of the law of property by Justinian, a Roman Emperor of the 6th century CE, to be very similar in many details to the Scots common law with which this book deals and which has built upon these, with some other, Roman law principles. What is missing from Justinian's treatment is the Roman lawyer's interest in litigation and the various types of action which were used to protect possession or transfer or to enable recovery of possession of property which the pursuer claimed he had become dispossessed (of which the most important was the action of *vindicatio*). What these actions serve to do is to point out that the distinctive quality of the Roman law was to define property in a context where the possession was always subject to possible threats. The manner of such threats and the manner in which facts were presumed or proved, and decisions made, have been an important element in the development of the law. Frequently, modern reforming legislation has failed to carry through the careful watchfulness of those who first laid out the principles in our own law and have thus created less than effective statutes.

While we do not discuss the historical Roman law, it will, however, be necessary when we consider land law to discuss the feudal system since, though now effectively abolished, the form of current land law documents and their clauses are very much dependent upon an understanding of feudalism, and this state of affairs will continue for some time to come.

PROPERTY, RIGHTS OF PROPERTY AND POSSESSION

Property

The word "property" is frequently rather confusingly used in two different senses: first, in the active sense of a right over a particular object and, second, in the passive sense of the object itself over which a right or rights exist.

Rights of property

In the active sense, Erskine defines property as "the right of using or disposing of a subject as our own, except in so far as we are restrained by law or paction" (*An Institute of the law of Scotland*, II, 1, 1). In this definition, Erskine is referring to the idea of the right of property ownership, the strongest right which it is possible for a person to have in a thing. But he asserts that this right, while appearing to be unrestricted, is in reality frequently subject to two different sorts of restriction: "paction" (by which Erskine means "agreement") and law. It is part of what we understand by ownership that the owner or possessor is entitled to use his property pretty much as the owner wishes and in particular to have the freedom to carry out normal acts in relation to the thing recognised by the law, namely to transfer, gift, loan, sell and pledge the item as security for a loan. All of these particular acts are recognised by law (they are termed "juridical acts") and are enabled by the law, but are within the control of the owner and thus are carried out by the owner where appropriate in agreement between the owner and third parties. Except in some circumstances, these juridical acts are carried out voluntarily by the owner. On the other hand, the law, while providing for the potency of these juridical acts of ownership, not merely giveth but also taketh away, and it is frequently our experience that our ownership of a thing is restricted by the operation of law. For example, we may not use our houses in *any* manner we wish (for example, we must have proper regard for our neighbours and avoid causing a nuisance); we must abide by the conditions of our tenure of the land laid down in our title deeds (for example, we may require to give such reasonable access to neighbours as is necessary to enable them to access their property or to carry out repairs on their property); and statutes may restrain us from doing certain things (so that we may not, for example, extend our property without obtaining any necessary planning permission and building control approval). There are many examples of this last type of statutory restriction of our rights.

In addition to rights of property ownership, there exists a whole raft of lesser rights in things. The law conveniently makes a distinction between rights in our own things and rights that we may have in the things owned by others. The former are referred to as *iura in re propria* while the latter are *iura in rei aliena*.

- *Iura in re propria* include the right to enjoy the fruits of ownership, the right to carry out the juridical acts referred to above, and, where appropriate, the right to consume the thing.

- *Iura in rei aliena* include servitudes (such as the right to have access over a neighbour's property), the right of a tenant under a lease, the right of a creditor in security (ie to take possession of an item pledged by the owner in security of a loan made to the owner and to sell the item and recover the proceeds should the owner default on the loan).

Possession

A person who has lawful ownership of a thing may (except where restricted as above) prevent all other persons from interfering with that possession. For example, an owner of land, finding that a neighbour is removing a mutually owned wall, may raise an action of declarator and interdict against the neighbour. The declarator establishes to the court's satisfaction the owner's right of ownership in the mutual wall and is a necessary prerequisite to the interdict which seeks an order from the court forbidding the neighbour from continuing the removal of the wall. After the order is granted, the neighbour will have to answer to the court if he continues in his unlawful removal of the wall.

Declarator in the above case is important, as the ownership of the wall must be established by reference to the pursuer's and defender's respective titles but, with many types of property, there is no need to have recourse to documents at all. Often the mere possession of an item of property is sufficient to establish lawful title to it. It is as a result of this presumption that it is sometimes said that "possession is nine-tenths of the law".

For many types of goods, the ownership of things will be presumed from possession of the thing. Possession is said to comprise two aspects: first, a physical element, and, second, a mental element (known as *animus possidendi*). The first element is easy to establish and simply involves who physically has control over the item. The second must be construed from the whole facts and circumstances of the case and involves whether the holder of the item intends to keep possession of it. For many purposes, a person has material possession of an item but not *animus possidendi*; for example, where an item being delivered to another is held by a carrier, the carrier has material possession of it ("custody") but has no mental intention to possess the item. The situation of a tenant is similar – he has occupation of the property but not ownership. There are therefore many situations in which the presumption of ownership will be rebutted in the whole facts and circumstances. To do so it is necessary to contradict the presumption by leading evidence to the contrary. But if no such evidence is led, the possessor will be regarded as the owner.

In the case of land and buildings, possession of property, even if not on the basis of an indefeasible title, can ripen into full ownership in certain circumstances and if the possession is in good faith. We shall return to this later. But at this stage we will observe that in the event that the possession is not in good faith (that is to say, the possessor has no proper grounds for belief that they lawfully possess the property) then the bad faith ("*mala fides*") possessor is not entitled to the fruits of the property, they are not entitled to recompense for any expenditure they may have spent in maintaining or improving the property, and indeed they may also be found liable to the true owner in damages for "violent profits". "Violent profits" means the maximum profits the true owner could have made if he had been in possession (sometimes described as the amount that the property might be made to yield by the "utmost industry" and, in the case of landed property, it has even been said to be twice the amount of rent that the property could have obtained, whether built upon or not).

Possession of property may be either *natural* or *civil*. "Natural" possession, as the word suggests, is the normal manner in which property is possessed, so that the owner of a house may occupy his property as his normal residence. "Civil" possession, on the other hand, involves possession through a representative, so that the owner of a house may lease the house out to tenants. The owner has civil possession of the house through the tenant for as long as the tenant continues to occupy the property.

CLASSIFICATION OF PROPERTY

Property in the other passive sense of the word, that of the objects over which rights exist, is classified as either *heritable* or *moveable*, and either *corporeal* or *incorporeal*. Heritable property means land and the buildings and other items of property physically attached to the land. Moveable property comprises every type of property that is not heritable. Thus, the two classes are mutually exclusive. The reason for this distinction is because of the importance of land as a social and economic value and because of the particular ways of proving ownership of land and of administering its transfer and succession. Corporeal property is property with a corporeal or physical existence. Incorporeal property comprises property that has no physical existence – usually it has a symbolic but socially recognised value. Examples are shares in a company, balances in a bank account, and so on. Again, these two categories are mutually exclusive. It follows that, taken together, these two categories of property result in four important different classes of property, which are considered in turn.

Corporeal heritable property

Corporeal heritable property is tangible (physical) heritable property which therefore includes not only land and buildings but also other fixtures attached to or comprising part of the land, for example crops, trees, stones, minerals etc. Such corporeal heritable property can therefore be possessed by the physical occupation of buildings and the use of the surrounding land. This occupation can be done by the owner of the land or by his tenants or employees or any other persons with the authority of the owner. Clearly, where a person occupies land, there is no guarantee that that person is the lawful owner. To establish ownership of corporeal heritable property, it is not enough simply to possess property, even where walls, fences and locks are used to keep others out. Ownership of corporeal heritable property requires proof of ownership by means of written documents of title which are registered or recorded to complete the ownership. Such titles will therefore necessarily involve a description of the interest in land possessed. Such a description will usually be by means of a verbal description of the surface boundaries or by means of a plan. Rights of ownership are deemed to project downwards all the way to the centre of the earth and to project upwards to the heaven above (the Latin maxim is "*a coelo usque ad centrum*"). As a result, the owner of the surface is, unless restricted, the owner of the rocks and minerals under the surface and is, unless restricted by law or contract, entitled to quarry the minerals and create mines within the property boundaries.

Certain important limitations are imposed on ownership of corporeal heritable property. For example, mines of gold and silver are the property of the Crown in terms of the Royal Mines Act 1424 and the Mines and Metals Act 1592, and the Civil Aviation Act 1982 allows aeroplanes to fly through what is, strictly speaking, property of the landowner.

Corporeal moveable property

All other tangible property is thus moveable. So, corporeal moveable property consists of goods in general. A strictly literal interpretation of "moveable property" is perhaps misleading, given that some property in this category is unlikely to be moved because of its size or weight. But in general corporeal moveable property comprises the sorts of things which can be physically taken and carried away and thus stolen. Title to corporeal moveable property usually depends upon proof merely of possession. However, proof of some categories of corporeal moveable may also involve documents of title. Some of these documents derive from the state authorities. Examples include the V5C vehicle registration certificate issued for road vehicles by the DVLA, aircraft registration certificates issued by the Civil Aviation Authority, and ship registrations issued by the UK Ship Register. In each of these cases the need for some form of official registration is caused by the very mobile nature of these forms of transport and is fulfilled by a central state authority. The documents of title may not, however, indicate the underlying ownership but merely the person who is the lawful keeper of the vehicle concerned and therefore responsible for the vehicle concerned. Thus it is the legal responsibility of the keeper of a road vehicle to ensure that that vehicle is taxed, has an MOT certificate and is insured if it is to be used on public roads. Other forms of valuable property may be sold along with certificates of a less formal nature, such as certificates of provenance of paintings, antiques and jewels. Their function is, however, primarily to provide an assurance of origin and authenticity rather than of title.

Incorporeal heritable property

In this category fall certain rights connected with land, but not being the land itself. Thus, leases and servitudes are incorporeal heritable property. We discuss both of these below. Also included are rights "with a future tract of time", such as pensions and annuities.

Incorporeal moveable property

This category contains rights which are not connected with land. In particular they include most of the important economic rights such as stocks and shares, bank deposits and intellectual property rights, for example copyright and patents (discussed further below). Some of these may involve documents of title, such as share and stock certificates and bank books. Others may involve no documents of title, such as intellectual property rights – though the rights may be perfected by entry into a public register, as is the case for patents, registered designs and registered trade marks.

Property incapable of private ownership

Excluded from the above categorisation are persons (*Reavis* v *Clan Line Steamers* (1925)), items such as air, the sea and running water (which are deemed in the law to be incapable of individual private ownership) and *res nullius* (items such as wild animals, which are ownerless until subject to *occupatio* (occupation or possession, discussed below)).

ORIGINAL ACQUISITION AND LOSS OF CORPOREAL MOVEABLE PROPERTY

Original acquisition of corporeal moveable property may be obtained by a variety of means.

Very often, rights are acquired by means of contract but very often the right is acquired by operation of law and that in the following ways:

Occupatio

Occupatio (or occupation), a Roman law term, is the doctrine whereby ownership is taken to property which was hitherto ownerless. The Latin maxim is *quod nullius est fit occupantis* – that which belongs to no one becomes the property of the taker. However, there is today a scarcity of property which can truly be said to be ownerless. Property which once had an owner, but which is lost or abandoned, will generally be owned by the Crown – *quod nullius est fit domini regis*.

Wild animals, birds and fish (excluding salmon, which are "Royal fish" and belong to the Crown) are thus susceptible to acquisition by occupancy if they are taken and controlled. It is permissible for any person to fish for and take wild trout and other fish in rivers and streams (provided that the activity of fishing is permitted by the riparian owners). This is because such fish are *res nullius*. However, in *Valentine* v *Kennedy* (1985) the accused were convicted of the theft of escaped rainbow trout which they had caught in a river outside the enclosure in which the trout had been kept. Although the fish had escaped, the sheriff held that ownership in them had not been lost. They could not be regarded as *res nullius* because the fish were not of a native species and, having been possessed, were capable of being stolen.

Specificatio

The doctrine of specification deals with the situation where a new thing has been created from materials which, at least in part, belonged to another, and where the other party's property cannot be restored to him in its original form. For example, if one person's grapes are made into wine, then a new product has been made and the original grapes cannot be restored to their former owner. Questions obviously arise as to the ownership of the new thing, and as to whether compensation is due to the party who has lost their original property.

The general rule is that the new thing belongs to the maker (Bell's *Principles*, 1289). In *International Banking Corporation* v *Ferguson Shaw & Sons* (1910), the defenders made lard from 53 barrels of oil which had been delivered to them. While the defenders were held to own the lard, they were required to pay compensation to the former owners of the oil. It should be noted that where a maker has acted in bad faith, he generally will not acquire a right of property in the manufactured product. In *McDonald* v *Provan of Scotland Street* (1960), it was argued that where a car had been made out of two other cars, one of which had been stolen, the maker could claim ownership of the resulting vehicle. In the event, the court held that specification did not occur (as it was possible to separate out the original parts of the new car) but that even if specification had occurred, then the maker would not have acquired ownership because of his bad faith.

Commixtio and *confusio*

Commixture is the mixing of solids, and confusion the mixing of liquids. Where either occurs, and the resulting property cannot be separated into its constituent parts, the result is co-owned by the owners of the constituent parts, according to the proportionate share or value contributed by each part. In *Tyzack & Branfoot Steamship Co* v *J S Sandeman & Sons* (1913) it was suggested that *commixtio* had occurred in relation to bales of jute.

Accessio

Accession occurs where two items of corporeal property become attached. The lesser item, known as the accessory, is subsumed into the ownership of the greater item (commonly known as the principal). The maxim is *accessorium principale sequitur* – the accessory follows the principal.

The principal effects of accession are as follows:

(1) separate ownership rights in the accessory are extinguished;

(2) the original ownership rights in the accessory do not revert to the original owner on subsequent separation;

(3) property may be converted from one class to another (see "The law of fixtures").

On attachment the owner of the principal becomes the owner of the whole including the accessory. Compensation may be due to the owner of the accessory but only where the attachment has been done by or on the instructions of the owner of the principal.

The law of fixtures

A special example of the idea of accession occurs when items of corporeal moveable property become annexed to heritable property such as land or buildings. This is an example of the principle of conversion where property of one class (corporeal moveable) is converted into another (heritable).

For example, when moveable property such as wood and bricks is built into a structure permanently fixed to the land, it ceases to be moveable and becomes heritable. In the case of *Brand's Trs* v *Brand's Trs* (1876), mining machinery (moveable property) was brought onto land leased by a tenant. On the tenant's death, the court held that the machinery had acceded to the heritable property owned by the landlord. What had been moveable had become a fixture upon the land. The intention of the parties was held to be irrelevant.

Under the common law, a number of recognised criteria exist which indicate where accession of moveable items to land and buildings may have taken place.

These include:

(1) degree of attachment;

(2) permanence of attachment;

(3) functional subordination;

(4) mutual special adaptation;

(5) time and expense of installation and removal;

(6) the intention of the parties.

These call for some individual explication:

Degree of attachment

The greater the degree of attachment to the ground, the more likely it is that accession will have taken place. However, it is important to note the existence of constructive fixtures such as the key of a door which, according to *Fisher* v *Dixon* (1843), is a fixture since the door into which it fits is heritable. In *Christie* v *Smith's Exr* (1949), a summer house weighing about 2 tons was held to be a fixture notwithstanding that it was merely resting upon the ground under its own weight rather than attached to it.

Permanence of attachment

Where moveable property is of a type where its installation is intended to be permanent, this indicates that they have acceded to the land. For example, in the case of *Scottish Discount Co* v *Blin* (1985), scrap industrial sheers (over 60 tonnes in weight) bolted to concrete foundations fell to be regarded as fixtures on the basis that when they were installed they were intended to be a permanent or quasi-permanent feature of the land to which they were attached.

Functional subordination

Where the accessory can be seen to serve the principal in some material way, it may be regarded as having acceded to the ground. For example, a central heating system fitted into a house will be regarded as a heritable fixture.

Mutual special adaptation

Where either the accessory or the principal has been adapted to fit the other, the accessory will be regarded as having acceded to the land. In *Howie's Trs* v *McLay* (1902), looms were placed in a shed the dimensions of which fitted the looms. The uppermost parts of the looms were bolted to the roof of the shed. The court held that the looms were heritable by accession. Similarly, if an item is designed to fit or match existing fixtures, it will generally also be regarded as a fixture. Where a painting is made to fit within panelling, it is likely to be regarded as a heritable fixture. However, as with all of these rules, there is some measure of ambiguity. In *Cochrane* v *Stevenson* (1891), the court had to consider a painting which had been incorporated into panelling. The painting concerned would have been regarded as a fixture except that it was merely one of a set of three paintings the other two of which were not so incorporated. The court held that because it was a member of a set, it would not be appropriate to hold that it had acceded in that instance.

Time and expense of installation and removal

The greater the time and expense involved in the installation of an item of moveable property, the more likely it is to be regarded as having acceded to the heritable property upon or into which it has been installed. A vehicle shredder which weighed 150 tonnes and took 3 months to install at a cost of £93,000 was held to have attached to the ground (*TSB Scotland plc* v *James Mills (Montrose) Ltd* (1991)).

The intention of the parties

Brand's Trs v *Brand's Trs* (1876) is authority for the proposition that the intention of the parties is not relevant in determining whether accession has taken place. Thus a contractual term that certain goods will remain moveable will have no effect where the criteria for attachment have been met. In *Shetland Islands Council* v *BP Petroleum Development* (1990), it was held that "no agreement between owner and occupier can affect the matter of ownership of heritable fixtures even as between them".

There are, however, several exceptions to this general rule. Where a tenant carries on business on property owned by his landlord, he is entitled to remove trade fixtures, that is property of the tenant which was attached by him for the purposes of his trade. The tenant's right of removal exists throughout the term of the lease, not just at its conclusion (*David Boswell Ltd* v *William Cook Engineering* (1989)). This is not to say that accession has not taken place, but only that the tenant is nonetheless entitled to removal. A similar rule exists in relation to agricultural tenants whose right of removal can extend to buildings (Agricultural Holdings (Scotland) Act 1991, s 18). Finally, industrial crops, that is those crops which require to be sown annually, are heritable as they are attached to the land. However, where a tenant has sown such a crop, he is entitled to reap and remove that crop.

Other forms of accession

While fixtures comprise the largest category, it is possible for accession to take place between two items of moveable property, or indeed two items of heritable property. Similar rules apply as regards ownership of the new piece of property.

There will not be accession of one moveable item to another unless it is impossible to separate the principal from the accessory without damage to one or other. In *Zahnrad Fabrik Passau Gmbh* v *Terex Ltd* (1986), it was held that where axles and transmissions had been installed in machinery, the test as to whether they had acceded was whether their efficiency had been reduced by removal, not whether there was a reduction in market value.

Accession of one piece of heritable property to another is rare, but may occur where a river, which forms the boundary between two properties, changes its course. If this happens gradually over a period of time it is termed *alluvio* and one landowner will benefit from the additional land which has been lost by the neighbouring proprietor. Seasonal variations, such as those caused by flood waters, are termed *avulsio*, and have no consequences for ownership. In *Stirling* v *Bartlett* (1992) the pursuer argued that a channel in the centre of a river which had been bulldozed 15 years previously should be taken as the boundary between his property and the defender's. The court held that this was not a case of *avulsio* and that the channel should accordingly be taken to be the boundary.

EXTINCTION OF RIGHTS IN MOVEABLE PROPERTY

Just as rights can be acquired in a variety of ways, so they can also be extinguished in a variety of ways. Rights may be assigned to others, or renounced. They may exist until the expiry of a term – for example, intellectual property rights are usually enforceable for only a fixed period. Or the item may be lost by accession, or indeed by destruction of the thing.

FURTHER GENERAL CONCEPTS

Real and personal rights

Rights in property can be further categorised as either real rights (*ius in re*) or personal rights (*ius ad rem* or *ius in personam*). The distinction is extremely important. A real right is a right in or over a piece of property, to use it, destroy it or have the right to its fruits. A personal right, on the other hand, is a right against another person which might be created by agreement or operation of law. It has long been recognised that real rights are the more valuable – they are enforceable "against the world" as opposed to personal rights which are enforceable against a person or persons.

> "... the essential difference may be perceived between rights that affect a subject itself, which are called real, and those which are found in obligation or, as they are generally styled, personal. A real right ... entitles the person vested with it to possess the subject as his own ... whereas the creditor in a personal right or obligation has only a *jus ad rem* or a right of action against the debtor ... but without any right in the subject" (*Erskine*, III, 1.2)

The case of *Muirhead & Turnbull* v *Dickson* (1905) illustrates the importance of the distinction between real rights and personal rights. The pursuers supplied a piano to the defender, who made some payments towards the total price. When the defender ceased making payments, the pursuers sued for delivery back to them of the piano, on the argument that the title (a real right) remained with them until the full price had been paid. Since the price had not been paid, they argued that they had retained ownership in the piano and were entitled to its return. However, the Court of Session decided that the transaction was properly to be construed as a credit sale, and that property (a *real* right) in the piano had passed when it was first delivered to the defender. Muirhead & Turnbull were thus left with a *personal* right to recover only the balance of the price.

You can see that rights of property constitute a bundle of rights in Scotland: more than one right may exist simultaneously over an item of property. For example, a house may be the subject of ownership, a standard security and a lease at the same time. Real rights are the fullest and most effective form of these.

Real rights

What, then, are the real rights which exist in Scots law?

The principal real right is "ownership". According to Erskine, ownership entails the right to use and dispose of property, subject only to any restriction imposed by the law or by agreement (II, 1.1). Subordinate real rights, *iura in re aliena,* exist where a person can enforce rights over the property in the ownership of another. Examples of subordinate rights include rights in security, leases, servitudes and simple possession. These will be considered in more detail later.

Personal rights

Personal rights, as the case of *Muirhead & Turnbull* v *Dickson* (1905) shows, are rights to demand the performance of a duty or obligation by another person. They may arise from contractual agreement or from the operation of law (for example, a person who breaches a duty of care can be obliged to make a payment of damages to the injured party). In the above case, the personal right was one of making payment of the outstanding amount in the agreement.

Property and ownership

It is, of course, possible for property to be owned by more than one person. Where this is the case, the property in question will be either common property or, much less frequently, joint property.

Common property

Common property describes the situation where an item is owned by more than one person, each of whom has a *pro indiviso* share in it. Shares are generally equal, but there is no requirement that this is so. Each co-owner has a right to a share of the whole property and to its use, but not to a particular part of it. Thus two co-owners of a house each have a one-half *pro-indiviso* share in the house. Each co-owner is entitled to dispose of their share without reference to the other. On death, the share of the deceased will pass to the deceased's heirs. *Pro indiviso* shares can be divided infinitely and there is therefore no limit to the number of co-owners that a piece of property may have. Each co-owner is entitled to further sub-divide their share. In addition it is open to any co-owner to raise an action of division and sale to enforce the sale of the property and the division of the proceeds.

There are various consequences of owning property in common. For example, what happens if there are co-owners of a house and it is necessary for the whole owners to undertake alterations and repairs to the house? In these circumstances, the general rule is that each co-owner is entitled to a say in the management of the common property. It is thus necessary to have the consent of all co-owners before repairs and maintenance can be carried out, unless the work is so minor as to be considered *de minimis* (*Rafique* v *Amin* (1997)). Where repairs are necessary, there is an important exception to the rule that unanimity is required: "Necessary repairs may be carried out by any one proprietor, and costs may be recovered pro-rata" (Bell's *Principles*, 1075).

The law in relation to the ownership of common parts within a tenement building has been altered by the Tenements (Scotland) Act 2004 (considered below), which removes the requirement for unanimity before work can take place.

Where there is agreement of all co-owners, any use of the common property is possible. However, where no such agreement exists, co-owners are limited to ordinary and reasonable uses.

Joint property

This form of ownership arises where two or more persons own property but do not have separate rights in it. The commonest example is where trustees own shares or other trust property, where partners hold partnership property, or club members hold the property of their club. They may not dispose of their rights to any other person either by a lifetime transfer or by will. In the event of their ceasing to hold the property, their right accresces to the other joint holders.

In the case of *Murray* v *Johnstone* (1896), a silver cup which was won by a club could not be given away against the wishes of a minority of the club members.

Common interest

This occurs where owners have individual rights to their own property but they must have regard to the interests of others arising in that property. For example, the owners of land through which a river flows ("riparian proprietors") have rights in common in the water flowing in the river. The corollary to this right is that the same riparian proprietors are under an obligation not to interfere with the natural flow of the water nor to exhaust the river of the water flowing in it. See also the law of the tenement (Chapter 5).

OWNERSHIP AND POSSESSION CONTRASTED

It can be seen from the above that the apparently simple concept of possession is not always straightforward. With items of corporeal moveable property of a small or moderate size, physical possession is possible but for most other forms of property, and in particular with property held in common or jointly, it is frequently necessary for there to be some means of formalising ownership in documents of title.

The obvious example of this is land ownership where a recorded or registered title is a prerequisite. But other documents of title may include stock and share certificates, bank books, car and aircraft registration documents, and the like. It does not always follow that the possession of a document of title necessitates ownership. Sometimes the underlying ownership is not that of the title holder but of some other party (for example, a car registration V5C indicates the name of the keeper who lawfully possesses the vehicle but the keeper may not be the vehicle's true owner).

While possession is a lesser right than ownership, possession of heritable property over a period of time can result in the attainment of ownership. This type of possession is sometimes referred to as "prescriptive possession" which is further discussed below.

Essential Facts

- **Origins of the law of property:** Scots property law derives from feudal law and from Roman law. This has been supplemented by statute.

- **Definition of property:** Erskine (*An Institute of the law of Scotland*, II, 1.1) defines property as "the right of using or disposing of a subject as our own, except in so far as we are restrained by law or paction".

- *Iura in re propria:* this is the name given to the rights which a person has in their own property. These include the right to enjoy the fruits of the property and to carry out the juridical acts of sale, gift, transfer and giving security.

- *Iura in rei aliena:* this is the name given to the rights which a person has in the property of another person. These include servitudes, interests of a tenant under a lease and interests of a creditor in a piece of property offered in security of the debt.

- **Possession:** this involves the physical element of custody and control over the item, and it also involves a mental element known as *animus possidendi*. Possession in bad faith ("*mala fides*") occurs where a person is not the true owner of property and is therefore not entitled to the fruits of the property. A *mala fides* possessor of property is liable to the true owner in violent profits – the maximum the true owner could have made if they had been in possession. Possession may be either natural or civil. Civil possession is possession carried out through a representative.

- **Classifications of property:** property is classified as either heritable or moveable, and either corporeal or incorporeal. This results in four different classes of property which are considered in turn.

- **Corporeal heritable property:** corporeal property is tangible (physical) property which means that it is capable of being physically possessed. Heritable property is land, with the buildings and other fixtures attached to the land, for example, crops, trees, stones, minerals etc. There are certain limitations imposed on ownership of corporeal heritable property. For example, mines of gold and silver are property of the Crown in terms of the Royal Mines Act 1424 and the Mines and Metals Act 1592; the Civil Aviation Act 1982 allows aeroplanes to fly through what is, strictly speaking, property of the landowner.

- **Corporeal moveable property:** all other tangible property is moveable. So, corporeal moveable property consists of goods in general. In general, corporeal moveable property comprises the sorts of things which can be physically taken and carried away and thus stolen. Title to corporeal moveable property usually depends upon proof merely of possession.

- **Incorporeal heritable property:** in this category fall certain rights connected with land, but not being the land itself. Thus, leases and servitudes are incorporeal heritable property.

- **Incorporeal moveable property:** this category contains rights which are not connected with land. In particular, they include important economic rights such as intellectual property rights, for example copyright and patents.

- **Property incapable of private ownership:** excluded from the above categorisation are persons, items such as air, the sea and running water (which are deemed in the law to be incapable of individual private ownership) and *res nullius* (items such as wild animals, which are ownerless until subject to *occupatio*).

- **Original acquisition and loss of corporeal moveable property:** there are a variety of means by which original acquisition of corporeal moveable property may be obtained. *Occupatio* is the doctrine whereby ownership is taken to property which was hitherto ownerless. Wild animals, birds and fish are thus susceptible to acquisition by occupancy if they are taken and controlled. It is permissible for any person to fish for and take wild trout and other fish in rivers and streams (provided that the activity of fishing is permitted by the riparian owners). This is because such fish are *res nullius*. *Specificatio* deals with the situation where a new thing has been created from materials which at least in part belonged to another, and where the other party's property cannot be restored to him in its original form. *Commixtio* is the mixing of solids, and *confusio* the mixing of liquids. Where either occurs, and the resulting property cannot be separated into its constituent parts, the result is co-owned by the owners of the constituent parts, according to the proportionate share or value contributed by each part. *Accessio* occurs where two items of corporeal property become attached. The lesser item, known as the accessory, is subsumed into the ownership of the greater item (commonly known as the principal). Separate ownership rights in the accessory are extinguished. The original ownership rights in the accessory do not revert to the original owner on subsequent separation. Property may be converted from one class to another (the "law of fixtures"). On attachment the owner of the principal becomes the owner of the whole including the accessory. Compensation may be due to the owner of the accessory. *Alluvio* occurs where one piece of heritable property accedes to another. This can occur where a river, which forms the boundary between two properties, gradually changes its course, adding to the land on one side of the river by deposition and taking away the land on the other by erosion. *Avulsio* occurs where seasonal variations, such as are caused by flood waters, and have no consequences for ownership.

- **The law of fixtures:** a special example of the idea of accession occurs when items of corporeal moveable property become annexed to heritable property such as land or buildings. This is an example of the principal of conversion where property of one class (corporeal moveable) is converted into another (heritable). For example, when moveable property such as wood and bricks is built into a structure permanently fixed to the land, it ceases to be moveable and becomes heritable. Under the common law, a number of recognised criteria exist which indicate where accession of moveable items to land and buildings may have taken place. These include:

  (1) degree of attachment;
  (2) permanence of attachment;
  (3) dunctional subordination;
  (4) mutual special adaptation;
  (5) time and expense of installation and removal;
  (6) the intention of the parties.

- **Incorporeal moveable property**: this means economic rights which include negotiable instruments, business goodwill and intellectual property rights. Negotiable instruments are tradeable documents giving evidence of claims for money against a debtor. The best-known forms are cheques. Business goodwill is the expectation that existing customers will return to a business, usually expressed in terms of a capital value of that expectation. A competitor who gains economic advantage by pretending to be associated with a well-known business may be liable to that business in damages for "passing off". The most important forms of intellectual property are copyright, patents, design rights and trade marks.

- **Real and personal rights:** rights in property can be categorised as either real rights or personal rights. A real right is a right in or over a piece of property, to use it, destroy it or have the right to its fruits. A personal right, on the other hand, is a right against another person which might be created by agreement or operation of law. *Real rights*: the principal real right is "ownership". Subordinate real rights exist where a person can enforce rights over the property in the ownership of another. Examples of subordinate rights include rights in security, leases, servitudes and simple possession. *Personal rights*: these are rights to demand the performance of a duty or obligation by another person. They may arise from contractual agreement or from the operation of law (for example, a person who breaches a duty of care can be obliged to make a payment of damages to the injured party).

- **Common property:** common property describes the situation where an item is owned by more than one person, each of whom has a *pro indiviso* share in it. Shares are generally equal. Each co-owner has a right to a share of the whole property and to its use, but not to a particular part of it. Each co-owner is entitled to a say in the management of the common property. It is thus necessary to have the consent of all co-owners before repairs and maintenance can be carried out, unless the work is so minor as to be considered *de minimis*. Where repairs are necessary, the Tenements (Scotland) Act 2004 lays out a scheme for management and apportionment of costs. Where there is agreement of all co-owners, any use of the common property is possible, however, where no such agreement exists, co-owners are limited to ordinary and reasonable uses.

- **Joint property:** this form of ownership arises where two or more persons own property but do not have separate rights in it. The commonest example is where trustees own shares or other trust property, where partners hold partnership property, or club members hold the property of their club. They may not dispose of their rights to any other person either by a lifetime transfer or by will.

- **Common interest:** this occurs where owners have individual rights to their own property but they must have regard to the interests of others which occur in that property. For example, the owners of land through which a river flows ("riparian proprietors") have rights in common in the water flowing in the river. The corollary to this right is that the same riparian proprietors are under an obligation not to interfere with the natural flow of the water nor to exhaust the river of the water flowing in it.

Essential Cases

Valentine v Kennedy (1985): in this case the accused were convicted of the theft of escaped rainbow trout (a domestic species) which they had caught in a river outside the enclosure in which the trout had been kept. Although the fish had escaped, the sheriff held that ownership in them had not been lost. Rainbow trout, unlike the native brown trout, could not be regarded as *res nullius* because the fish were not of a native species and the trout in question, having once been possessed, were capable of being stolen.

International Banking Corporation v Ferguson Shaw & Sons (1910): in this case the defenders made lard from 53 barrels of oil which had been delivered to them. While the defenders were held to own the lard, they were required to pay compensation to the former owners of the oil.

Fisher v Dixon (1843): this case related to the degree of attachment. A door was held to be a fixture since the doorway into which it fits is heritable.

Christie v Smith's Exr (1949): this case related to the degree of attachment . A summer house weighing about 2 tons was held to be a fixture even though it was merely resting upon the ground under its own weight rather than attached to it.

Scottish Discount Co v Blin (1985): this case related to permanence of attachment. Scrap industrial sheers (over 60 tonnes in weight) bolted to concrete foundations fell to be regarded as fixtures on the basis that when they were installed they were intended to be a permanent or quasi-permanent feature of the land to which they were attached.

Howie's Trs v McLay (1902): this case related to the adaption of the items. Looms were placed in a shed, the dimensions of which fitted the looms. The uppermost parts of the looms were bolted to the roof of the shed. The court held that the looms were heritable by accession.

Cochrane v Stevenson (1891): a painting incorporated into panelling would have been regarded as a fixture except that it was part of a set of three paintings and the two others had not been so incorporated and so the first painting was held not to have acceded to the building.

Zahnrad Fabrik Passau Gmbh v Terex Ltd (1986): axles and transmissions were installed in machinery. The court held that if these items would be reduced in their efficiency on removal, then they had acceded to the machinery. In this way the court insisted that they would have acceded unless their identity and use as axles and transmission were unaffected by removal, in which case they would not be regarded as having acceded.

Stirling v Bartlett (1992): the channel of a river bed which had been bulldozed was held not to have been subject to avulsion and so the bulldozed channel could not be taken as the boundary.

Shetland Islands Council v BP Petroleum Development (1990): in this case the intention of the parties was held to be irrelevant: "No agreement between owner and occupier can affect the matter of ownership of heritable fixtures even as between them."

Muirhead & Turnbull v Dickson (1905): this illustrates the importance of the distinction between real rights and personal rights. The pursuers supplied a piano to the defender, who made some payments towards the total price. The pursuers sued for delivery back to them of the piano. The court held that the transaction was a credit sale and so a real right of property had passed to the defender when it was first delivered to him. Muirhead & Turnbull were left with only a *personal* right against the defender to recover the balance of the unpaid price.

Murray v Johnstone (1896): in this case a silver cup which was won by a club was held to be joint property and so could not be given away against the wishes of a minority of the club members.

2 INTELLECTUAL PROPERTY RIGHTS

Incorporeal moveable property is perhaps the most important of all the rights in moveable property as the values which are expressed and recognised by the law express important social or more commonly economic interests.

Examples of this include: bank deposits and accounts (where the receipt or bank book showing the amount of the deposit is a certificate of title to the deposit); stocks and shares in a company (where the owner has rights to shares or periodic payments in the company provided for in the articles of association of the company and evidenced by certificates issued by the company's registrars); negotiable instruments (where the document is a personal obligation to pay money payable to the *bona fide* holder a title to demand payment – for example, bearer bonds).

Among the most important of these incorporeal moveable rights are the various intellectual property (IP) rights which we now summarise.

COPYRIGHT

Copyright is the legal right to prevent others from copying or reproducing an individual's creative work in such a way as to take advantage of the creator's right to exploit the work economically. Copyright, as with all IP rights, is mainly about protecting an owner's commercial interests in creative work.

To understand copyright, we have to understand the kinds of work which are protected.

First, it is not the idea itself which is protected but rather it is the expression of a creative idea that is protected. It is only when an idea has been rendered in a fixed form, such as being committed to paper or being recorded on tape or disk or on film or otherwise, that it can be protected. The fixed form which is protected varies from one type of work to another.

The ideas themselves, rather than the expression of the idea, are not protected and anyone can acquire and use knowledge which they have obtained from a copyright work. That means that they cannot be stopped from borrowing an idea or even from producing their own work which is very similar to that of the original creator.

Copyright in a creative work arises automatically and does not require any formal set of procedures or registration. This means that as soon as a piece of creative work has been fixed in its form then the individual who has created it is entitled to protect the work and provided in law with the means of doing so. However, there may be difficulties in doing so, since to protect the work, the original creator must prove that they have authorship of the item. This may mean that they have to produce the original fixed copy and evidence of the time when the work was created or fixed into its final form and published. This information may be readily available: for example, where an author has written a book which is published the publication date can be clearly established by the copyright notice on the back of the title page. In other cases it may be that the author has to avail themselves of some recording service in order to protect their copyright work. In this way a third party certifies what exactly constitutes the protected work and when it was fixed.

The statute providing copyright protection in the United Kingdom is the Copyright, Designs and Patents Act 1988, as amended. As with most intellectual property rights, British protections are very similar to those available across Europe and further afield as a result of a number of international agreements and conventions and European Union Directives

Historical background

The first English copyright system was created in 1556 when authors were able to register their printed books with the Stationers Company in London. The system did not apply to Scotland, which was a separate jurisdiction at the time, and as a result books were imported here from England and other foreign countries and reprinted in Scotland. The justification for the reprinting was that it was considered here that all Scottish people should have the right to acquire knowledge and learn from reading the works of citizens of other countries and this caused no problems until the early part of the 18th century. When Scotland and England became one united kingdom there was no restriction in Scottish reprinted books being sold in England and this was seen as Scots making money out of English authors. It became necessary for there to be one copyright law for the whole United Kingdom. This was achieved by the Statute of Anne of 1710 which gave authors a renewable copyright period of 14 years and thus protected statutorily for the first time an author's right to prevent others from copying and profiting unfairly from the author's books. The statute contains a number of innovations. For example, copyright transmitted to the representatives of deceased persons. Another feature of the Statute of Anne was that it created a number of copyright libraries. It is still the case that the major British libraries are entitled to receive one copy of all books published here in the UK.

Since 1710, the class of works which are protected has extended from printed books to include a very wide range of materials. A large leap forward was made in the Berne Copyright Convention of 1885 which set out to codify intellectual property copyright protections across the Convention states. In the 1970s there were a number of significant reforms, and in 1988 the current statute was enacted.

The 1988 Act deals not only with copyright, but also with related rights, moral rights of authors, performer's rights, and unregistered design rights (which we will come to later). Some specialist rights, such as semiconductor topography rights, have become protected by subsequent EC Directives.

The principal type of copyright protected works are what are known as "primary" or "authorial" works, or perhaps better as "LDMA" works. These are:

- literary works;
- dramatic works;
- musical works; and
- artistic works.

There are also what might be called "entrepreneurial", "secondary" or "derivative" works which are:

- sound recordings;
- films;
- broadcasts; and
- typographical arrangements of published editions – the typography right in facsimile editions.

We will first look at what these primary or LDMA works consist in. These works are defined in the early sections of the 1988 Act (ss 3 and 4).

Literary works

These are published works consisting of words – whether written, printed, spoken, sung or otherwise displayed or recorded.

The statutory definition is given in s 3(1) of the 1988 Act as:

" 'literary' work means any work, other than a dramatic or musical work, which is written, spoken or sung, and accordingly includes –

(a)   a table or compilation other than a database;

(b)   a computer programme;

(c)   preparatory design material for a computer programme; and

(d)   a database."

In *University of London Press Ltd* v *University Tutorial Press Ltd* (1916), a tutorial college, catering for students intending to sit the University of London's external examinations in mathematics, printed copies of the University of London's past exam papers. It did so without the permission of the University. The University claimed copyright in the questions. In defence, the Tutorial Press argued that the ideas involved in the questions were mathematical ideas well known to most mathematicians and so the questions could not be "original works" and therefore were not capable of copyright protection. The court disagreed and said that it was necessary for literary works to be "original" in the sense of the expression of the ideas on the paper but not in the sense of the ideas themselves being original. The exam questions as they appeared in the papers were an original expression of mathematical ideas and so the papers were protected as "original works". Infringement had taken place.

From this case we can see that the work is not "literature" in the sense that we might use the term of a classic novel but that it simply consists of words or other features which are written or printed or otherwise reproduced. The courts have decided that a literary work must be the product of the creator's skill, labour and judgement, and in particular that it must have some merit, impart some instruction, information or pleasure. This is an important definition.

It follows from this definition that single words or the titles of films are not copyright protectable unless they are of sufficient length, inventiveness, entertainment or instruction as to indicate creative merit.

Another important case is that of *Ladbroke (Football) Ltd* v *William Hill (Football) Ltd* (1964). This case showed that something as mundane as a football pools coupon could be regarded as an original literary work in the sense that it involved skill and labour in the design.

As a result, we can see that literary works include all books, magazines, newspapers, published articles, poems and so on, whether in fact, written, printed or displayed electronically (say, on the Internet).

In recent times it was not clear whether this included printed circuit diagrams or whether those should better be regarded as artistic works. A recent case held that there is no reason why literary and artistic copyright could not reside in the same work.

It should be noticed that the copyright owner also has rights in derivative works such as transactions in translations of the original work.

Dramatic works

The statute defines dramatic works as including "a work of dance or mime" (s 3(1)). This skeletal definition has some odd consequences. For example, the performance of a song by somebody dressed up in costume would not be a dramatic work but would be a literary or musical work. So, how have the courts interpreted "dramatic"?

They have tended to interpret dramatic works as being works of action capable of public performance.

Even this has been problematic. In the case of *Norowzian* v *Arks Ltd (No 2)* (2000), an advertisement film producer used a technique of editing and composing film frames called "jump cutting". The resultant film (*Anticipation*) showed a man apparently dancing in a quirky jerky fashion while waiting for a pint of Guinness to settle. The plaintiff claimed that this breached the copyright in a film called *Joy* that he had made in 1992 using the same technique. In the court of the first instance, the English High Court, it was held that the film was not a dramatic work since the dancing was the product of a film-editing technique and was incapable of being actually performed by an individual on a public stage. However, on appeal, the Court of Appeal held that a dramatic work could include a film made by jump cutting because the film could be performed publicly before an audience. The court said that the dramatic work was "a work of action with or without words or music which is capable of being performed before an audience" and that this test was satisfied in this case.

Musical works

"Music' is not defined in the statute (s 3(1) merely says that "'musical work' means a work consisting of music, exclusive of any words or action intended to be sung, spoken or performed with the music") and so we may have to use a dictionary definition. A useful such definition of "music" may be "the art of combining vocal and/or instrumental sounds in a harmonious and expressive way; the printed or written score of this; a pleasant natural sound".

In another case, *Lawton* v *Dundas* (1985), it was held that Channel 4's signature tune was a protected musical work even though in fact it consisted of only four notes.

So it seems that both musical scores and the distinctive music that is performed from them can be regarded as musical works in the ownership of the original composer. We shall see later that authorised recordings of musical works also give rise to secondary rights known as recording rights and there are performer's rights which authorised performers may have in their own performances.

Note that several copyright rights can exist in the same work at the same time but be held by different people. For example, a recording of a song will involve the literary copyright of the author of the lyrics; the musical copyright of the composer of the music; the performers' rights of the singers and the band; and the recording producer's rights in the sound recording.

Artistic works

The statute defines these very widely and says that these include graphic works, photographs, sculptures or collages (all irrespective of artistic quality) and also works of architecture (being buildings, models for a building, or designs for buildings) and works of artistic craftsmanship. Just as for literary works, it should be noticed that the first group of artistic works are protected irrespective of artistic quality. This has given rise to number of cases.

There has been a tendency away from protecting every type of artistic work under copyright. Where a design is clearly intended to fulfil a commercial purpose it is less likely to be protected as a copyright work.

In *Antiquesportfolio.com Plc* v *Rodney Fitch & Co Ltd* (2001), the court held that the photographer of a photographic work showed artistic craftsmanship in his choice of subject-matter, lighting, positioning and camera angle. What appears to be essential in any artistic work is that the work demonstrates the original skill, labour and experience of the artist concerned.

Sound recordings

A "sound recording" is defined in the statute as a recording of sounds from which sounds may be reproduced; or a recording of the whole or any part of a literary, dramatic or musical work from which sounds reproduced in the work may be reproduced. The statute goes on to say that this is regardless of the medium in which the recording has been made. There is no requirement for originality. The soundtrack attached to a film is now regarded as part of the film.

Films and broadcasts

These are defined as "a recording in any medium from which a moving image may be, by any means, reproduced". This definition therefore includes video, television and movies and also stills from these. Film rights also extend to the sound rights recorded with a film. A "broadcast" is defined as "a transmission by wireless telegraphy of visual images, sounds and other information".

In both of these cases the copyrights concerned are derivative rights resting in the producers of the film or broadcast. It should be noted that the author also has rights in broadcast work and can prevent copying so that the film and broadcast rights can derive only from authorised productions.

Infringement – the restricted acts

What counts as restricted acts are defined in ss 16 *et seq* and include:

- copying;
- issuing copies to the public;
- rental or lending to the public;
- performing;
- showing or performing the work in public; or
- broadcasting.

You will notice that these are all economic exploitations of the original protected work. It is this protection of economic interests in creative works which intellectual property rights generally cover.

For an infringement to be upheld, it is essential that it should be shown that there has been copying or another restricted act of the whole or a substantial part of the protected work.

The courts need to know what constitutes a substantial part and in *Designers Guild Ltd* v *Russell Williams Textiles Ltd* (2001), the court gave a number of pointers. For example:

- substantiality was measured qualitatively and not quantitatively; and
- the opposite of substantial is insignificant;

- in determining substantiality no weight is to be given to anything that is commonplace, well known, or derived from another source (ie not original);

- the court also said that the object of copyright law is to protect the product of the author's skill and labour and was not there to create an economic monopoly in the idea underlying the work.

Typographic arrangements

These are also protected, as we have seen, and it is an infringement to make facsimiles of existing typographic arrangements. But facsimiles mean an exact copy of the original page layouts.

In *Newspaper Licensing v Marks & Spencer* (2003), the store collated and reproduced certain newspaper cuttings taken from a press agency. It was held this was not an infringement of typography rights because such an infringement would require the exact reproduction of the page concerned. The court held that "nothing short of a facsimile copy would suffice".

Adaptations

Adaptations are also protected and these relate to literary, dramatic and musical works. An adaptation of a literary and dramatic work will include a translation, a conversion of a dramatic work into a non-dramatic format and vice versa, the reproduction of a work in the form of the story conveyed by pictures for inclusion in a book, a musical or a magazine, and so on.

In relation to musical works, "adaptation" means an arrangement or transcription.

In relation to computer programs, "adaptation" means the conversion of the program from one computer language to another.

Secondary infringement

This is governed by ss 22–26 of the Act and concerns items (which are the products of primary infringement) which are then imported into the United Kingdom for commercial exploitation here.

Possessing or dealing or distributing infringing copies is secondary infringement.

It is also secondary infringement to permit premises or apparatus to be used for an infringing performance.

The principles of secondary infringement are carried across to include copy protection devices and s 296 prevents the importation sale, hire, or advertising of a device which is designed or adapted to get around legitimate copy protection devices. Technological copy protection systems are sometimes referred to as Digital Rights Management (DRM). These involve any digital method of preventing the end user from accessing, copying or converting a protected work. DRM is much favoured in the entertainment industry and sets out to be a technological method of protecting the copyright of films, games, music and other copyright materials. The justification for these devices is that in an age where most household have personal computers, it is all too easy to download and copy copyright materials and that the substantive law, while making such copying unlawful, actionable or even criminal, is actually unable to provide an effective means of protection. In an age of iTunes and iPods, it is often difficult for teenagers to understand that copying copious quantities of music is illegal. DRM attempts to provide a technical rather than a legal method of preventing this abuse. However, against these justifications of DRM are the arguments that social conditions have changed and that non-commercial copying of tracks for home use on an iPod is not a threat to the entertainment industry.

Note that it is not secondary infringement to buy a legal copy of a copyright work elsewhere in the world and then to import it into the United Kingdom, provided that this is done only for private and domestic purposes.

Remedies

The remedies open to the owner of copyright works include:

(1) injunction or interdict (including interim injunction or interdict) to prevent restricted acts from being repeated by the infringer;

(2) declarator: the decree in which the court find and declares whether there has been infringement;

(3) damages: that the copyright owner can obtain compensation for loss of opportunity to exploit the work commercially – usually related to loss of sales; though the measure can be the amount the court finds would be reasonable amount of royalties for the grant of a licence had that been applied for by the infringer;

(4) accounting for profits: where the court requires the infringer to produce evidence of any profit he has made from the infringements;

(5) order for delivery of infringing copies: obtaining the court's authority for the recovery and destruction of any infringing material;

(6) power to press for criminal proceedings: most of the rights open to copyright owners will also have associated criminal offences.

In addition to the above there are criminal offences for communicating a copyright work. The criminal law aspects of copyright are pursued, investigated and prosecuted by the trading standards authorities.

Defences: statutory fair dealing exemptions – the "permitted acts"

Because of the balance between the rights to acquire knowledge and the right of an owner to exploit their creation economically, there exist a number of permitted acts which permit the dissemination of ideas but do not prevent the author from exploiting the work economically.

For example, a few articles in a book may be photocopied for research and private study, but substantial photocopying, such as would be likely to prevent the author from obtaining a sale of the book, would not be permitted (s 29). Other permitted acts allow the copying of passages for criticism, review and reporting of current events (s 30), certain educational uses (ss 32–36), and other permissions exist for certain acts by libraries, archives, public administration and judicial proceedings (ss 37 *et seq*).

Moral rights

In addition to copyright protections, which are economic rights, there are also the moral rights of the author or creator.

There are three types of moral rights:

(1) the "paternity right" of the author to be identified as such;

(2) the "integrity right" of the author to object to derogatory treatment of the work (a deletion, alteration or adaption which distorts or mutilates the work or would be prejudicial to the honour and reputation of the author would breach this integrity right);

(3) the right not to have the work falsely attributed.

These are not economic rights, except that integrity right can have economic consequences.

Performance rights

A performer in public, providing that he is authorised to perform the work in question, has the right to say who may record the performance and for what purposes it may be recorded.

Recordings require consent. The kinds of things which qualify are dramatic and musical performances, readings and recitations of literary works, variety, circus and comedy acts. Recording rights in a performance are usually embodied in exclusive recording contracts with the performer.

Copying for private and domestic use are generally exempt and permitted acts.

A performer's property rights are threefold:

(1) *reproduction* right: the right to copy the recording;
(2) *distribution* right: the right to issue recordings to the public;
(3) *rental and lending* right: the right to rent or lend a recording to the public.

It can be seen that these are rights to economic remuneration derived from a performer's performance.

Duration of protection

In the main, copyright in the LDMA works will last for 70 years after the death of the original creator. Film rights last for 70 years from the death of the principal director. Sound recording and broadcast right last for 50 years from the time when the recording was released.

Copyright in typographical arrangements lasts for 25 years from the year when the edition was first published. Performance rights last for 50 years from the time when the performance took place.

Moral rights, which require to be asserted by the author, generally subsist as long as a copyright subsists but false attribution right subsists until 20 years after the creator's death. Moral rights are the only copyrights which require to be positively asserted.

PATENTS

Patents are the oldest form of intellectual property rights. There are very early examples where the Crown gave monopoly rights to favoured individuals by Letters Patent. In the early days these were not restricted to inventions. It slowly became clear that Crown patronage was being abused and so by the Statute of Monopolies of 1623 certain limits were placed upon letters patents and the rights which followed from them. Gradually, patent law developed into the form in which it exists today. The current statute is the Patents Act 1977, as amended.

General

A patent is a monopoly right lasting for 20 years (25 years in the case of pharmaceutical patents). The Patents Act states that what is protected is a product or process which satisfies certain criteria:

(1) it must be new or novel;

(2) it must involve an inventive step;

(3) it must be capable of industrial application; and

(4) it must not be excluded.

Generally, the excluded things are (by s 1(2) and (3)):

(1) a discovery, scientific theory or mathematical method;

(2) a literary, dramatic, musical or artist work or any other aesthetic creation;

(3) a scheme, rule or method for performing a mental act, playing a game or doing business, or a computer program;

(4) the presentation of information;

(5) certain biotechnological inventions which are detailed in Sch 2A to the Act

The biotechnological exclusions are excluded on the basis of public policy and morality. They involve such matters as the human body in its various stages of formation and development, human cloning, human genetic identity modification processes, the use of human embryos from industrial commercial purposes, plant and animal varieties (which may have other forms of protection such as the Plant Varieties Act 1997), the genetic modification of animals such as are likely to cause material suffering without any substantial medical benefit (an example of a case where this was argued is the *Harvard Onco Mouse* (1991)).

The "as such" rule

The exclusions in s 1(2) and (3) prevent patents from being obtained in excluded matters "as such". These matters cannot be patented. But this does not disallow patents which take advantage of the technical application or contribution of excluded matters. For example, an invention which achieves a definite purpose and industrial application can be patented even when it does so by including an excepted matter having a technical contribution to the invention. This does not appear to extend to excluded biotechnological matters.

As a result of the "as such" rule, in *Merrill Lynch's application* (1989), a program on a computer which enabled markets to be created was held as unacceptable for patenting because the program had the purpose of a method of doing business (which is an excluded matter). It was argued that it would not necessarily have been excluded on the basis of being a computer program, since that had technical effect. But it was the use of the computer program to perform a method of doing business which was excluded. The use of a computer program as such is not patentable but the use in a patent of a computer program to achieve a necessary technical effect does not prevent a patent from being granted providing the end result performs some purpose that is not excluded. In Merrill Lynch's case the patent was unacceptable because it was still a means of doing business – another excluded matter.

Another related issue is that there is continuing consultation in the EU about whether and under what conditions the European Union should allow computer programs and business methods to be patented, as they currently can be at present in the United States (albeit under some restrictions). It is thought that by having a markedly different regime in the EU, this may mean that businesses which would otherwise prosper here, might migrate to the USA where their computer program and business method inventions can be patented and a commercial monopoly obtained there.

Novelty

This requirement is defined in the statute as meaning that what is to be patented must not already be part of the "state of the art" nor must it have been made available to the public anywhere in the world in any way. Clearly, on any patent application being received it must be judged by asking whether the invention is novel by reference to the state of the art at the time of the application.

Disclosure of the invention which would make it part of the "state of the art" can be carried out in a number of ways. The three ways are in particular:

(1) *publication*: where the invention and the way that it is used has been disclosed to the public in published sources, journals, books, articles, or even where the inventor has made disclosures by demonstrations of the invention. These disqualifying publications can occur anywhere in the world and will prevent a patent from being regarded as a novel;

(2) an *earlier patent application* (even if only a few days earlier) will prevent a later application which uses the same technology from being regarded as novel. However, the earlier application must contain "enabling information" which means that it must disclose sufficiently how the patent works and also how it is to be applied and used;

(3) *use*: the principle is that it is not proper to apply for and obtain a monopoly where the product or process is something which is or has already been made or done by other people. A very good example here is the case of *Windsurfing International Inc* v *Tabur Marine (GB) Ltd* (1985) which involved a 12-year-old boy who had anticipated Windsurfing International's wishbone spar surfboard patent application by having used the same type of surfboard in public a number of years prior to the application. The court was able to view a film of his early use of this off the Isle of Wight. The disclosure meant that the invention was sufficiently well known as to be unprotectable by the patent application.

Earlier uses will not necessarily disqualify an invention unless the disclosure is sufficient to provide information about how the invention works and is applied or used ("enabling disclosure") so that in the case of *PLG Research Ltd* v *Ardon International* (1995) the earlier use did not disqualify.

Inventive step

An invention is required to show an inventive step which is "not obvious to a person skilled in the art, having regard to any matter which forms part of the state of the art". This requirement is set out in s 3. This has given rise to a number of questions about what is "obvious" and what is not. Two cases are important here:

(1) *Technograph Printed Circuits Ltd* v *Mills & Rockley (Electronics) Ltd* (1972) which held that the person to whom a patent must be obvious is "a skilled but unimaginative worker". Obviously, the requisite level of skill and imagination will vary from application to application.

(2) *Windsurfing International* (again) in which four principles were stated by the court to identify an inventive step and these are:

    i. identify the inventive concept;

    ii. what was the general knowledge in the state of the art at the priority date (date of application)?

    iii. what is the difference between the matter cited in the alleged invention and the general knowledge in the state of the art at the priority date?

    iv. are these steps obvious to the skilled man?

It can be seen that this gives rise to a number of issues. Courts have often asked why, if something is obvious, it has not been done before. This is known as the problem of hindsight. In *Haberman & another* v *Jackel International Ltd* (1999) this involved the "any way up" cup used by babies. The problem was that babies often dropped what they were drinking and spilt the contents of their cups. The invention provided a solution to this problem which was that the cup had a very small slit in the mouthpiece which allowed water and other liquids to escape only when there was sucking action: when the cup was dropped the liquids wouldn't spill out. This was the first patent application to deal with this particular problem.

Ownership

The ownership is usually vested in the inventor but there are exceptions to this. One very important category of exception relates to employees. Usually if a person is employed as an inventor, the patents in the inventions will accrue to the employer. But not all inventions invented by employees will be owned by the employer. Employers will have rights in an invention where the invention is made in the course of the employee's normal employment duties. It is therefore important to look to the employee's contract of employment to decide whether or not they are required to invent in order to fulfil their duties. In other cases, it will be necessary to look at a number of other criteria which may indicate that the employer expects invention rights to accrue to them.

Applications

When a person wishes to have a patent, they must make an application on the prescribed form and they must include a number of documents. These documents are:

(1) the *abstract*: this is a very brief description of the invention and how it works. The reason for the abstract is to give some notice in the *Official Journal* at the time when the application is first lodged;

(2) the *specification*: which contains the technical drawings and technical description of the patent stating how the patented article or process is made and how it works and what its functional components are;

(3) the *claim*: these are the legal description of what it is claimed as a monopoly.

In *Catnic Components Ltd v Hill & Smith Ltd* (1982) which involved a lifting device with a vertical load bearing component. An alleged infringer had a closely similar device for load lifting but which had a slightly inclined load-bearing component 6 degrees off the vertical. The court had to decide whether or not the variant was materially different for if it was then there would be no infringement.

DESIGNS

Industrial designs are protected in a number of ways of which the most important are United Kingdom Registered Designs and United Kingdom Unregistered Designs. For both of these there are European counterparts which vary slightly but depend on much the same principles.

Traditionally, copyright was the most important source of protections in the design field but, as we have seen, the courts have moved away from protecting (as primary artistic works) purely commercial designs and instead are more concerned to protect genuine aesthetic creations. It is partly for that reason that a separate "design right law" is required to protect industrial designs.

Definitions

In any design right law there is a practical question about what kinds of features are appropriate for a registered protection and what kinds of things are appropriate for unregistered protection. Naturally, the statute that creates these protections have definitions to which we can refer.

A registered design right covers (Registered Designs Act 1949) "the appearance of the whole or part of a product resulting from the features of, in particular, the lines, contours, colours, shapes, texture or materials of the product or of its ornamentation" (s 1(2)). What is protected by registered designs then are aspects of the appearance of the article.

Unregistered designs are covered by ss 213–264 of the Copyright, Designs and Patents Act 1988 have a different definition. Unregistered design protection extends to "any aspect of the design, shape or configuration, internal or external of the whole or part of an article". This means the shape of a product or its configuration, including internal workings, may be protected even if the protected features are invisible to the human eye or totally enclosed within the article. It can be seen that this makes unregistered design rights much more important for protecting the functional or technical aspects of a product rather than the aesthetic appearance.

Exclusions

There are a number of things which are excluded from protection as design features. Among these the most important are "must fit" and "must match" exclusions.

- *"Must fit"* features occur where aspects of the shape or configuration are required (forced upon the design) to enable the article to be connected to, placed in, around, or against another article in order that the design product can perform its functions. As a result, that part of the design is not something which is purely the creative product of the designer. Instead it is something which the designer has had to design around. Such features cannot be protected.

- *"Must match"* features occur where the shape, or configuration of parts of the design are dependent upon the appearance of other articles to which the design product is associated. For example, where a piece of electronic equipment is made to have the same dimensions, colour and visible design features as other associated products. Again, such features are not the product of the designer's creative thinking but are features that the designer must incorporate. These aspects of the design cannot be protected.

TRADE MARKS

One of the difficulties with trade marks is how they are to be defined. In the Trade Marks Act 1994, s 1 defines a trade mark as "a symbol or sign placed on, or used in relation to, one trader's goods or services to distinguish them from the goods or services supplied by other traders". The statute then goes on to say that the sign must be capable of being represented *graphically*. This is presumably because the trade mark rights generally arise by way of registration. The trade mark application must adequately specify the distinctive mark which is to be used. Note again that trade marks may be registered or unregistered (arising by exclusive usage in the relevant sector of trade). Unregistered marks are an automatic right arising from trade usage by the owner.

Trade mark protections historically arose in the mid-19th century when it became clear that maker's marks applied to goods could become distinctive and have an intrinsic value. It was clear that there was a need of some form of legal recognition and protection.

Note also that, even if unregistered, a trade mark can be protected under the common law of passing off. This means that if somebody attempts to pass themselves off as being another trader by the use of that other trader's mark, then the infringer's activities can be stopped. "Passing off" means that the infringer is effectively taking advantage of the goodwill owned by the principal business. The difficulty in the case of unregistered trade marks is that proof must be given of the use of the mark, that the mark is unique or a least well known in the trader's distinctive sector, that the mark is recognised by consumers and other traders, and that the infringer has used the mark to gain sales on the basis of confusion with the goods of the owner of the mark. Clearly, registering a trade mark avoids these four additional items of proof.

Trade marks have a number of well-known functions:

(1) they may allow goods to be differentiated and therefore enable recognition by consumers;
(2) they may be a guarantee of quality;
(3) they may protect traders and consumers;
(4) they may provide a guarantee of origin.

Given the definition in the 1994 Act, it is perfectly possible to trade mark words and particular typefaces of words but in addition there have been some notable areas of dispute. The courts have therefore built up a considerable body of case law. In particular issues have occurred with the following:

- *Shapes*: these can be protected (for example, the Coca-Cola bottle) but there may be good reasons not to do so. In *Philips Electronics NV* v *Remington Consumer Products* (2002), the court refused to protect a three-head arrangement of an electric razor, on the basis that this would grant "its proprietor a monopoly on technical solutions or functional characteristics of a product which a user is likely to seek in the products of a competitor". It is clear that shapes which are chosen as a trade mark for aesthetic or other ancillary reasons can be protected, while shapes which are an intrinsic requirement of the product cannot be protected, as that would give an unreasonable advantage to the company claiming the trade mark in the shape.

- *Colours*: this is particularly important with drug capsules which may become well known by consumers from their colours and shapes (for example, the Viagra pill). But in recent times there have been cases such as *Orange Personal Communications Ltd's application* (1998) where an attempt to trade mark a particular shade of orange was refused on the ground of insufficient specification. The court held that since there were "unaccountable different numbers of shades" that the use of the expression could refer to under the wide generic name of "orange", this did not provide sufficient information to state what precisely was protected.

- *Sounds and smells*: the need for a graphic representation has produced some difficulties with these as well. It has been held that in many cases musical notation is sufficient to protect a sound (for anyone who knows, the notation will be able to read from it the type of sound that is protected), but there are difficulties where the trader seeks to protect natural sounds which cannot be reduced to musical notation. In the case of smells, there are difficulties in specifying these. Individual chemical scents can be uniquely identified from their chemical formulae for a chemist can theoretically go away and reproduce the chemical in his laboratory and so see what it smells like. But even a chemist is unable to gain an insight into the smell from reading the formula alone. The issue for both sounds and smells, then, is how a graphic description can be made specific enough for it to be understandable to the educated reader and so utilisable as a trade mark. This is not to say that a verbal description is impossible but cases show how difficult it is. In *Venootschap onder Firma Senta Aromatic Marketing's Application* (1999), an application was made to register the "smell of fresh cut grass" as a trade mark for a tennis balls manufacturer. The court held that the issue is always "whether or not this description gives a clear enough information to those reading it to walk away with an immediate and unambiguous idea of what the mark is ... the smell of fresh cut grass is a distinct smell, which everyone immediately recognises from experience ... the Board is satisfied that the description provided for the olfactory mark sought to be registered for tennis balls is appropriate and complies with the graphical representation requirement". But in *John Lewis's application (scent of cinnamon)* (2001) an attempt to obtain a trade mark for the scent of cinnamon was refused. In most cases the chemical formula of the scent and even a sample of the chemical will be insufficient since this will not enable a person reading the graphical description to get any idea of what the trade mark is.

The essence of the trade mark sign is that it must be capable of distinguishing goods and services of one business from those of another. This is not necessarily a high standard but it will obviously bar the use of any signs which are incapable of adequate specification, graphic representation and those that are physically incapable of functioning as a distinctive sign associated with products.

Any mark which is void of distinctive character is also excluded, as are any that are exclusively descriptive or generic (like the use of "personal" if applied to personal computers) as these, like the technical and functional shapes referred to above, would give an unfair advantage to the trade mark owner.

Signs that are exclusively descriptive

It is not permissible to use as a trade mark something which is a general description for the goods or services concerned such as would indicate kind, quality, quantity, purpose, value, geographical origin and other characteristics. It is not possible to register signs likely to offend or deceive or which are contrary to public policy. There are also prohibited emblems such as indicators of Crown patronage, the use of national flags, or the Olympic symbol. Nor is it allowed to use signs in bad faith.

For registered trade marks, the process of registration involves the completion of an application form giving certain prescribed information about the identity and address of the applicant, a statement of particular product or service to be protected, a graphical representation of the mark, and the statement that the mark is already being or is about to be used by the applicant. In addition the applicant needs to pay the fees for each class of goods or services it is intended to use the mark with. Schedule 4 to the Trade Marks Rules 2000 gives 34 classes of goods and 11 classes of services which may be identified in the application.

Following the application, a search and examination is made and notification of the application is published. If no opposition is filed, the application will be granted. The grant of a trade mark satisfies the property assertions which we have seen before and which have to be proved with an unregistered trade mark when raising an action of infringement.

PASSING OFF

Unlike the previously discussed forms of intellectual property, passing off is the product of common law rather than of statute. The idea of passing off is that one business falsely trades upon confusion of their goods and services with those of an established competitor. That is to say they trade on the goodwill of the competitor in order to obtain sales. This is likely to have two effects: first, a reduction in the competitor's sales; and second, harm to the competitor's reputation.

Goodwill is a quantifiable asset of a business. Just as the investment of money in investments will produce a quantifiable return on capital employed (ROCE) – higher where the capital is employed in a business which is a going concern – so the level of turnover derived from goodwill can be capitalised (based on the amount of return you can get on capital employed in a business in the sector concerned) and the product shown as an asset in the firm's balance sheet. Brands and trade marks can be valued in the same sort of way and can also appear in the balance sheets of businesses as assets. Hence, the results of passing off, which results in the filching of the firm's customers and a downturn in turnover, is quantifiable in capital terms as a loss of goodwill. The value of this capital loss may represent a good estimate of the amount of damages done to a firm by such passing off activity.

Passing off essentially occurs with the reputation of party A is misappropriated by party B, such that party B misrepresents this reputation and damages the goodwill of party A. We have seen the dynamics of this above.

The three fundamental elements to passing off are therefore:

(1) *Reputation*: a business must have built up a trade reputation recognised by customers and rival businesses. Sometimes this can be built up quickly. In *Stannard* v *Reay* (1967) a mobile fish and chip van, "Mr Chippy", had built up a protectable goodwill after only 3 weeks. In addition, goodwill can be very localised or it can be global. In the case of the chip van, the goodwill was very localised in character. But other businesses may have a national or global market and reputation.

(2) *Misrepresentation*: the infringer must intend to misrepresent their products as that of the established product in order to filch sales from the producer of the established product. This can be done by using

the mark or name of the established product, copying the design or shape of the established product, generating confusion by the use of a similar name, or similar advertising or in other ways. The ultimate issue is whether this has been done in order to confuse the public.

(3) *Damage*: the third element is that the established business has been damaged by the infringer's activities. That is to say, it has lost customers and hence its goodwill has been damaged.

Another related topic is the phenomenon of cybersquatting which occurs where individuals (cybersquatters) register Internet domain names indicating a connection with an established business. In *British Telecommunications plc v One in a Million Ltd* (1999), the defendant company had registered a large number of domain names such as "ladbrokes.com", "sainsbury.com", "marksandspencer.com", "bt.org" and a host of others. The court held that the defendants were passing themselves off as the much better-known public companies and that there was an attempt to cash in on the goodwill of the better-known companies. Often cybersquatters register these names in order to attempt to sell the domain names to the better known companies rather than to obtain sales from those companies by fraudulent trading. But such name sale attempts are still highly objectionable. Today there is an alternative procedure for removing cybersquatters. It is open to an aggrieved business to request the Internet Corporation for Assigned Names and Numbers (ICANN) to adjudicate on the matter and cancel the offending bad faith registration.

CONFIDENTIAL INFORMATION

Although not strictly an issue of intellectual property, confidential information can be regarded as owned by a business (and may also be protected in other circumstances too). Confidential information should not be confused with individual privacy which has protection under the Human Rights Act 1998 and elsewhere.

Some companies prefer to keep their trade secrets secure rather than to rely on any other type of intellectual property. There may be many reasons for this. One of these is that a successfully kept trade secret can give a company an advantage for a long period of time until the secret becomes known. There are many examples: Coca-Cola, Glayva whisky liqueur, Baxter's soups and sauces and Tunnock's caramel wafer biscuits. These are all products which are prepared using a trade recipe which is kept as a secure trade secret. The Coca-Cola recipe has remained secret since its invention in 1886. It is said that it originally contained "sugar crystals, caramel, caffeine, phosphoric acid, coca leaf, kola nut extract, lime extract, vanilla, glycerin and a secret ingredient known as 'merchandise 7X' ". It has clearly been to the company's trade advantage to preserve its secret for a very lengthy period. It would not have been able to maintain their advantage had the recipe been merely patented, for it could then have been copied after the 20-year monopoly had expired.

Trade secrets occur wherever a business holds and utilises price-sensitive or commercially sensitive information. This is likely to be divulged to employees on a "need to know basis" in the course of employment. Very often this includes the names of suppliers and customers. But a trade secret occurs wherever there is information which a business can use to gain commercial advantage over its competitors who do not hold the information. Trade secrets are therefore very broad in their scope. It is clearly of importance to ensure that employees realise that the information is a trade secret and that they should not divulge it (often a business will require its employees to enter into confidentiality agreements – but this may not be necessary).

The law recognises many other specific different categories of confidential relationship. For example, the law recognises and protects personal secrets between a husband and a wife, secrets between friends, drawings by members of the Royal Family, state secrets, the privileged relationships of professional confidentiality, and information imparted in circumstances of confidence.

The general legal protections were best summarised in the case of *Coco v A N Clark (Engineering) Ltd* (1969). Here, the court stated that there were three requirements which had to be proved before the court would intervene:

(1) the information must have the quality of confidence;
(2) the information must have been imparted in circumstances implying an obligation of confidence; and
(3) the information must have been used without authority.

The case concerned a claimant who had designed a moped engine but needed a prototype to be built. He therefore opened discussions with the defendants who were an engineering company who the plaintiff wanted to build the engine. To enable the negotiations the plaintiff divulged the details of the design in full but a confidentiality contract was never negotiated finally. When the parties fell out, the defendants decided to produce their own engine which very closely resembled the claimant's. He claimed that the discussions had been confidential and that therefore the defendants, the engineering company, were not entitled to exploit the information they had received. In the end the court held that only the second requirement had been proved and the plaintiff was unsuccessful in his claim.

Another requirement is that the information concerned should not already be in the public domain or otherwise known generally. In the case of trade secrets, this will very often cover technical information such as the mechanics of an invention or a recipe for a product, as well as customer and supplier and financial information. Such secret information can be protected if it is detailed enough to enable another party to exploit it, but this does not apply if it is simply a general method or scheme held by one party.

Even after confidential information is in the public domain, it does not imply that a person to whom it has previously been divulged in confidence may make use of it. This feature of confidential information is what is called the "springboard doctrine". This was referred to in the case of *Terrapin Ltd* v *Builders Supply Company* (1967), where the defendants had made prefabricated units for the plaintiffs' buildings. During the period of the confidentiality agreement they had full details of the design of these fabricated units. After the agreement ended, the defendants produced their own buildings, using prefabricated units very similar to those produced by the plaintiffs. Not surprisingly, the latter claimed a breach of confidence. The defendants argued that any member of the public could inspect the plaintiffs' buildings at any time and that such inspection would reveal the previously secret design details and that therefore these details were in the public domain or potentially in the public domain and so, the confidentiality agreement having ceased, they, like anyone else, were entitled to exploit the design. The court, however, decided that since the original information in a highly specified form had been released to the defendants in a relationship of confidence, it followed that although the public might be able to utilise the information, obtaining it by inspection, a person to whom it had been disclosed in confidence continued to be held under an obligation for a reasonable period thereafter and could not exploit information to the detriment of the original owner.

Another issue raised by the case of *Coco* v *A N Clark* (1969) involves what characterises a relationship of confidence. This has been stated to be based on any of contract, trust, friendship and also on recognised legal relationships of marriage and so on. The contractual type agreements are most likely to occur in the field of business negotiations and may be either express or implied.

In the case of non-contractual relationships, certain categories are well recognised: there are the confidential relationships between doctors and patients, lawyers and clients, and bankers and customers (all of these must divulge the confidential information if required to do so by law or by a court).

Finally, before damages can be granted, the information must have been used in an unauthorised way to the detriment of the plaintiff or to the advantage of the defendant. Both of these outcomes will be of relevance in the ascertainment of damages.

Defences

One important defence is that of public interest. An example of this is the case of *Lion Laboratories Ltd* v *Evans and Others* (1984) where employees in the business which created "Lion Intoximeter" breath alcohol analysing devices used by the police discovered that there were certain circumstances in which those devices gave false readings. These employees were concerned that this might give rise to people being falsely convicted of drink-driving where these particular conditions had by chance occurred. The company, Lion Laboratories Ltd, wanted to keep this information secret as it might affect confidence in its products, but the employees felt that they had to divulge the information to the press in the public interest and in the interests of justice. They did so and the court held that they were, in so doing, entitled to take advantage of the defence of public interest.

Essential Facts

- **Copyright:** copyright protects the fixed expression of an idea. It is not the ideas themselves which are protected. Copyright is protected in the UK by the Copyright, Designs and Patents Act 1988 as amended. Copyright works are categorised by the form in which they occur. Primary works, or authorial works, comprise literary, dramatic, musical and artistic works. Secondary, or entrepreneurial works, include sound recordings, films, broadcasts and typographical arrangements.

- **Literary works:** means "any work, other than a dramatic or musical work, which is written, spoken or sung". The emphasis is on the words which are protected. As a result literary copyright includes the lyrics of songs, the words of a dramatic work, and also tables and computer programs (which are lists of coded instructions).
- **Dramatic works:** includes "a work of dance or mime" which has been interpreted to mean "a work of action with or without words or music which is capable of being performed before an audience".
- **Musical works:** "'musical work' means a work consisting of music, exclusive of any words or action intended to be sung, spoken or performed with the music". The work has to have some original merit but it has been held that this may consist of merely four notes.
- **Artistic works:** these include graphic works, photographs, sculptures or collages (all irrespective of artistic quality) and also works of architecture (being buildings, models for a building, or designs for buildings) and works of artistic craftsmanship. The work should demonstrate the original skill, labour and experience of the artist concerned.
- **Restricted acts:** the following acts constitute primary infringement if done without the copyright holder's permission: copying the work; issuing copies to the public; rental or lending to the public; performing the work; showing or performing the work in public; or broadcasting.
- **Secondary infringement:** this involves importing the products of primary infringement into the United Kingdom for commercial exploitation here. It includes possessing, dealing or distributing such infringing copies. Section 296 of the 1988 Act prevents the importation sale, hire or advertising of a device which is designed or adapted to get around legitimate copy protection devices.
- **Remedies:** the remedies which copyright holders can obtain from the courts are: interdict/injunction; declarator; damages; accounting for profits; order for delivery and destruction of infringing copies; and the power to prompt relevant criminal proceedings. These remedies also occur in relation to most other forms of intellectual property claims.

- **Statutory fair dealing:** Certain non-profit-making acts do not constitute infringements of copyright, provided they are non-substantial and are not likely to prevent the copyright holder from obtaining a normal reward for their work. The permitted acts include small amounts of copying for research, private study, criticism, reviewing and reporting current events, certain educational activities and certain activities necessary in relation to libraries, archives, public administration and judicial proceedings and the like.

- **Moral rights:** these are non-economic rights relating to an author's right to identified as such, the right to object to derogatory treatment of a work and the right not to have the work falsely attributed. These rights require to be asserted.

- **Performance rights:** when permitted by an author, a performer may perform a work in public and has rights over the recording of the performances and the distribution and economic exploitation of such recordings.

- **Duration of copyright protection**: LDMA copyright lasts for 70 years after the death of the original creator. Film rights last 70 years from the death of the principal director. Sound recording and broadcast rights last for 50 years from the release or broadcast. Performance rights last 50 years from the performance. Rights in typographical arrangements lasts 25 years from publication. Moral rights last until 20 years after the creator's death.

- **Patents:** a patent is a monopoly right lasting for 20 years (25 years in the case of pharmaceutical patents). Patents are regulated by the Patents Act 1977, as amended, and if an invention is to be protected, a patented product or process must be: new or novel; involve an inventive step; be capable of industrial application; and must not be an excluded matter. The excluded matters include works that are protected under copyright; discoveries, scientific theories, mathematical methods; schemes, rules and methods for doing a mental act, playing a game, doing business, or a computer program; the presentation of information; and certain biotechnological processes. The "as such" rule may allow a patent to be protected where the invention includes excluded matters which make a technical contribution to the operation of the invention.

- **Patents: novelty:** since a patent has to be novel, any enabling disclosure (a disclosure which shows how the invention works) will prevent a product or process from being patented. As part of the application process, searches are conducted to assess novelty. Any publication, use, or disclosure anywhere in the world will count against novelty if the disclosure is enabling.

- **Patents: inventive step:** an inventive step must not be "obvious to a person skilled in the art, having regard to any matter which forms part of the state of the art". This raises the question of hindsight. What may be obvious in hindsight may not have been obvious at the time of the patent application. Another approach which tries to avoid hindsight, is to ask whether there was a real problem which the invention solved for the first time. If so then the invention appears to involve an inventive step and was not obvious at the time even if it appears so in hindsight on the basis of what we now know.

- **Designs:** Design rights protect industrial designs. UK Registered designs are regulated by the Registered Designs Act 1949 and protect "the appearance of the whole or part of a product resulting from the features of, in particular, the lines, contours, colours, shapes, texture or materials of the product or of its ornamentation" (s 1(2)). The test for this is the appearance of the external design features. This was at one time referred to as the "eye test". Unregistered Design Rights are regulated by ss 213–264 of the Copyright, Designs and Patents Act 1988 and extend to "any aspect of the design, shape or configuration, internal or external of the whole or part of an article". This means that UDR can protect the internal configuration of an industrial article and not merely its aesthetic appearance.

- **Designs: "must fit" and "must match" exclusions:** those aspects of the design which are not within the designer's freedom of choice are not parts of the design which are capable of protection. As a consequence, if the article requires to be designed to fit in, against or around another item, those parts which must be designed to fit are not capable of protection. In a similar way, where features of the shape or configuration of the design are dependent upon the appearance of other articles to which the design product is associated, those features are not capable of protection.

- **Trade marks:** s 1 of the Trade Marks Act 1994 defines a "trade mark" as "a symbol or sign placed on, or used in relation to, one trader's goods or services to distinguish them from the goods or services supplied by other traders". The statute then goes on to say that the sign must be capable of being represented *graphically*. It is this insistence on the possibility of graphical representation which produces some curious consequences when the protection of shapes, colours, smells and sounds is considered. It is not permissible to use as a trade mark something which is a general description for the goods or services concerned such as would indicate kind, quality, quantity, purpose, value, geographical origin and other characteristics. It is not possible to register signs likely to offend or deceive or which are contrary to public policy. There are also prohibited emblems such as indicators of Crown patronage, the use of national flags, or the Olympic symbol. Nor is it allowed to use signs in bad faith.

- **Passing off:** this occurs where one business falsely trades upon confusion of their goods and services with those of an established competitor. In creating confusion, the first business hopes to steal sales away from the established competitor. Such activity is controlled by the common law. There are three elements to a passing-off action: (1) the established business must have an established reputation to protect; (2) there must have been a misrepresentation by the infringing company; and (3) the established business must have been damaged by the infringer's activities – usually by loss of sales.

- **Confidential information:** the common law recognises certain definite circumstances where there are protections against the leak of confidential information. The most obvious of these concerns the protection of trade secrets where price-sensitive and commercially sensitive information are jealously guarded. The law requires three elements of confidential information to be proved before passing off is declared. Those elements are: (1) the information must have the quality of confidence; (2) the information must have been imparted in circumstances implying an obligation of confidence; and (3) the information must have been used without authority. Information in the public domain is not confidential. Where information has been imparted in confidence and subsequently becomes known in the public domain, the person to whom the confidential information was imparted is not entitled to profit from it to the detriment of the original owner. This is called the "springboard doctrine".

Essential Cases

University of London Press Ltd v University Tutorial Press Ltd (1916): a tutorial college printed copies of the University of London's past exam papers. It did so without the permission of the University. The University claimed copyright in the questions. The Tutorial Press argued that the ideas involved in the questions were mathematical ideas well known to most mathematicians. The court held that it was the original expression of the ideas as exam questions which was protected and not the underlying mathematical ideas themselves.

Ladbroke (Football) Ltd v William Hill (Football) Ltd (1964): this case showed that something as mundane as a football pools coupon could be regarded as an original literary work in the sense that it involved skill and labour in the design.

Norowzian v Arks Ltd (No 2) (2000): this case involved a short advertising film made using a "jump cut" technique. Although the dancing in the film could not be performed by a dancer (the action in the film was the product of the editing of the frames), the work was still a dramatic work as it was a work of action which could, as a film, be performed in public.

Antiquesportfolio.com Plc v Rodney Fitch & Co Ltd (2001): held that the photographer of a photographic work showed artistic craftsmanship in his choice of subject-matter, lighting, positioning and camera angle. What appears to be essential in any artistic work is that the work demonstrates the original skill, labour and experience of the artist concerned.

Merrill Lynch's application (1989): involved a program on a computer which enabled markets to be created was held as unacceptable for patenting because the program had the purpose of a method of doing business (which is an excluded matter).

Windsurfing International Inc v Tabur Marine (GB) Ltd (1985): a 12-year-old boy had anticipated Windsurfing International's wishbone spar surfboard patent application by having used the same type of surfboard in public a number of years prior to the application. The court held that this enabling use had disclosed the invention which therefore could not be regarded as novel.

Technograph Printed Circuits Ltd v Mills & Rockley (Electronics) Ltd (1972): this case held that the person to whom a patent must be obvious if it is to breach the inventive step rule should be "a skilled but unimaginative worker".

Haberman v Jackel International Ltd (1999): involved the "any way up" cup invented to be used by babies. The problem was that babies often dropped what they were drinking and spilt the contents of their cups. The invention provided the solution which was that the cup with a very small slit in the mouthpiece which allowed water and other liquids to escape only when there was sucking action. This meant that when the cup was dropped the liquids wouldn't spill out. The invention appears obvious in hindsight, but it was the first solution to this problem. No one had thought of this solution before.

Philips Electronics NV v Remington Consumer Products (2002): the court refused to protect a three-head arrangement of an electric razor on the basis that this would grant "its proprietor a monopoly on technical solutions or functional characteristics of a product which a user is likely to seek in the products of a competitor".

Venootschap onder Firma Senta Aromatic Marketing's Application (1999): an application was made to register the "smell of fresh cut grass" as a trade mark for a tennis balls manufacturer. The court held that the issue is always "whether or not this description gives a clear enough information to those reading it to walk away with an immediate and unambiguous idea of what the mark is ... the smell of fresh cut grass is a distinct smell, which everyone immediately recognises from experience ... the Board is satisfied that the description provided for the olfactory mark sought to be registered for tennis balls is appropriate and complies with the graphical representation requirement".

Stannard v Reay (1967): a mobile fish and chip van, "Mr Chippy", had built up a protectable goodwill after only 3 weeks. In addition, goodwill can be very localised or it can be global. In the case of the chip van, the goodwill was very localised in character. But other businesses may have a national or global market and reputation.

Coco v A N Clark (Engineering) Ltd (1969): the claimant had designed a moped engine but needed a prototype to be built. He therefore opened discussions with the defendants who were an engineering company who the plaintiff wanted to build the engine. To enable the negotiations the plaintiff divulged the details of the design in full but a confidentiality contract was never negotiated finally. When the parties fell out the defendants decided to produce their own engine which very closely resembled the claimant's. He claimed that the discussions had been confidential and that therefore the defendants, the engineering company, were not entitled to exploit the information they had received. In the end the court held that only the second requirement had been proved and the plaintiff was unsuccessful in his claim.

Terrapin Ltd v Builders Supply Co (1967): the defendants had made prefabricated units for the plaintiffs' buildings. During the period of the confidentiality agreement they had full details of the design of these fabricated units. After the agreement ended, the defendants produced their own buildings using prefabricated units very similar to those produced by the plaintiffs. Terrapin claimed a breach of confidence. Builders Supply argued that any member of the public could inspect the plaintiffs' buildings at any time and that such inspection would reveal the previously secret design details and that therefore these details were in the public domain or potentially in the public domain and so, the confidentiality agreement having ceased, they, like anyone else, were entitled to exploit the design. The court, however, decided that since the original information in a highly specified form had been released to the defendants in a relationship of confidence, that it followed that although the public might be able to utilise the information, obtaining it by inspection, a person to whom it had been disclosed in confidence continued to be held under an obligation for a reasonable period thereafter and could not exploit information to the detriment of the original owner.

Lion Laboratories Ltd v Evans (1984): employees in the business which created "Lion Intoximeter" breath alcohol analysing devices used by the police discovered that there were certain circumstances in which those devices gave false readings. These employees were concerned that this might give rise to people being falsely convicted of drink-driving where these particular conditions had by chance occurred. The company, Lion Laboratories Ltd, wanted to keep this information secret as it might affect confidence in its products, but the employees felt that they had to divulge the information to the press in the public interest and in the interests of justice. They did so and the court held that they were, in so doing, entitled to take advantage of the defence of public interest.

3 RIGHTS IN SECURITY

STAGES IN TRANSFER OF PROPERTY AND THE POSSIBILITY OF SECURITY

When a party decides to transfer their interest to another there are usually three stages involved:

(1) *Contract of sale*: where the seller and the purchaser together form an agreement (have *consensus in idem*) to sell the item and so agree on the price and any other conditions of sale. A set of personal rights and obligations are undertaken (which the parties can enforce against each other);

(2) *Assignation*: where in the case of either incorporeal moveable property or heritable property the sale agreement is given effect in a written document which transfers the title from the seller to the purchaser;

(3) *Delivery*: when the item (in the case of corporeal moveable property) or the written document of assignation (representing the property) is delivered up to the purchaser, thus denuding the seller of their interest in the property. This has the effect of giving the purchaser real rights in the property which can be defended against any other person. In the case of heritable property, the delivery is then completed by registration in the appropriate public register.

It follows that this arrangement brings about the possibility of deposit of an item or of documentation representing it to a creditor in security of a loan to a debtor owner of the property. Thus, when an owner of property borrows money he is undertaking a personal obligation to repay the sums borrowed together with interest. If the debtor fails to make payment, the creditor must raise a court action for payment of the outstanding amounts. However, to make sure that payment is made, a creditor often seeks security for the loan and interest by requiring that the debtor deliver up to the creditor some article of value in security for the loan. In the event of the debtor's default or bankruptcy, if the creditor has a real right in the property delivered to them, it can sell the property to secure payment of the debt. If the proceeds are sufficient to settle the debt in full then any excess of proceeds is returned to the debtor or his trustee in bankruptcy.

In the event of there being insufficient funds to pay the debt in full, then the creditor becomes an ordinary unsecured creditor on the estate of the debtor for the balance due.

In many cases this delivery is no more than a power to take possession of the property in the event of default in payment. But the idea of delivery such as to create a real right in favour of the creditor, or something equivalent to delivery, is the key to understanding the idea of rights in security. The Latin maxim is *traditionibus, non nudis pactis, dominia rerum transferuntur* – real rights in property are transferred by delivery and not merely by agreement.

EXCEPTIONS TO THE RULE CONCERNING DELIVERY – FLOATING CHARGES AND HYPOTHECS

There are two exceptions to the general rule concerning delivery. These are (1) floating charges and (2) hypothecs. In both of these cases there is security without possession.

Floating charges

Floating charges depend upon statute for their efficacy. For an explanation of the way in which floating charges can give security over heritable property in Scotland, see p 68 below. Companies in Scotland since 1961 (Companies (Floating Charges) (Scotland) Act 1961, as amended by the Companies Act 1985 and the Companies Act 2006) have been able to grant a floating charge over their whole assets (heritable and moveable alike). The floating charge requires to be registered with Companies House in the company's file held there. Because floating charges can range over the whole of a company's assets, including its stock, a security which required delivery would be impossible. Every time a secured item of stock were to be sold this would necessitate a formal release by the creditor. Instead, a floating charge does not attach to any particular assets until a prescribed event such as a winding up occurs. On such event, the floating charge "crystallises" and attaches to the whole assets of the company. As a result, a floating charge is a very flexible form of security and is ideally suited to trading corporate businesses. Floating charges in Scotland now have to be registered not only in the charges section of the company's file held by Companies House but also in the Register of Charges kept by the Keeper of the Registers of Scotland.

Hypothecs

These are types of security without delivery which arise in a number of specified commercial situations. They are commonly classified into "conventional hypothecs" and "legal hypothecs". Conventional hypothecs arise from contract. They are the creation of maritime commerce and involve rights in security granted by the master of a ship in the event of an emergency to raise funds to enable a voyage to be completed. If the security is limited to the cargo of the ship then the hypothec is a "bond of respondentia". If the security extends to the ship itself then the hypothec is a "bond of bottomry". There are a number of legal hypothecs; including the right of a solicitor to look to his client's costs and property recovered in a court action to secure unpaid expenses due to the solicitor (solicitor's hypothec for the costs, now provided for by the Solicitors (Scotland) Act 1980, s 62), the right of a landlord to look to his tenant's possessions to secure unpaid rent (landlord's hypothec for rent), and the right of the master and seamen to look to the ship for security for unpaid wages (maritime hypothecs, now provided for by the Merchant Shipping Act 1995, ss 39 *et seq*). The area of hypothecs is complex and specialised.

RIGHTS IN SECURITY OVER MOVEABLE PROPERTY – PLEDGE AND LIEN

Rights in security over moveable property where delivery is needed to create a real right may be achieved by pledges or deposits (these two are created by express contract) or liens (implied by operation of law).

Pledge

With pledge, the pledger contracts to borrow money and agrees to deliver over to the pledgee the item of moveable property in security for the personal obligation. On fulfilment of the obligation, the pledgee must deliver the property back to the debtor. Delivery is therefore essential to the contract. Delivery may be:

(1) *actual* (when the property is physically transferred);

(2) *constructive* (for example, where the goods are held in a store, and the owner gives an instruction to the storekeeper instructing him to hold the goods for and if appropriate to deliver the goods to the pledgee – in which case the giving of the intimation to the storekeeper is an essential for the creation of a real right in favour

of the creditor. It is essential for delivery that the storekeeper is an independent person from the pledger and not, for example, an employee of the pledger); or

(3) *symbolical* (for example where a bill of lading, being a symbol for goods shipped, is delivered to the pledgee. This delivery of the bill of lading is regarded in law as an effectual symbolical delivery of the goods themselves and so is capable of creating the real right in security).

Pledges are very common as a means of giving security for loans. For example, the ubiquitous pawn-broker who gives small and short-term loans to the impecunious who deposit their items of value in the hope of redeeming them – but often are unable to do so. Pledge is, however, useful for bank loans too and it is not uncommon for debtors to deliver stock and share certificates to their bank along with a blank signed stock transfer form which can be used by the creditor to sell the stocks and shares in the event of default. Life assurance policies may also be deposited or formally assigned to a creditor. Under Scots law a pledge of a life assurance policy is incomplete until a formal assignation has been signed and delivered to the creditor and the creditor has given notice of the assignation to the life company. The assignation procedure gives the creditor a real right in the policy. It follows that when the loan is repaid, the assigned policy requires to be re-assigned (retrocessed) to the assured and a notice of the retrocession is given to the life company, reinstating the assured as the person entitled to the benefits under the policy (returning to the assured the real right to the policy). However, the practice of banks has become lax due to dilution by the English practice of simple deposit (which merely gives a personal and therefore incomplete right to the creditor).

Liens

Liens are rights implied by law to hold on to moveable property owned by another until that other has satisfied their debt or other obligation owed to the holder. Liens may be special or general.

A special lien involves a single contractual transaction and entitles a person holding the property to retain it until the obligation constituted in the contract is fulfilled. An example of this is where a carrier is instructed to carry goods. The carrier is entitled to hold onto the goods and not deliver them up until his fee for the carriage is paid. This is a special lien because it is restricted to property held in relation to that particular transaction. A carrier does not have a special lien over other property held in relation to other transactions with the same debtor.

A general lien entitles the person holding the property to hold it generally in security for all obligations owed by the debtor. Usually this involves some general balance of money owed for a course of dealing involving a number of separate transactions. There are four generally recognised forms:

(1) lien of *factor*: who has a general lien over all goods, documents and money owned by the principal and coming into the factor's possession in the course of his dealings with the principal;

(2) lien of *banker*: who has a general lien over bills of exchange, cheques, promissory notes and other similar negotiable instruments belonging to the customer and coming into the banker's possession in the course of his banking dealings with the principal. The lien does not extend to items deposited with the banker for safe keeping;

(3) lien of *solicitor*: who has a general lien over all documents including title deeds and share certificates deposited by the client. The lien is to secure all professional fees and expenses made in the ordinary course of business on the client's behalf. A solicitor is not, however, entitled to dispose of the property and may only retain it until payment. The solicitor must produce the property if it is required in a court action. Where a client has become bankrupt, the solicitor must hand the property over to the client's trustee but will thereafter be ranked as a preferred creditor on the bankrupt's estate.

(4) lien of *innkeeper*: who has a general lien over the luggage of a guest to secure the amount owed for hotel bills.

RIGHTS IN SECURITY OVER HERITABLE PROPERTY – STANDARD SECURITIES

The law providing for heritable securities was considerably reformed by the Conveyancing and Feudal Reform (Scotland) Act 1970. The Act replaced all previous forms of heritable security with one simple and very flexible basic form: the standard security.

At its simplest, the minimum wording required to create a standard security is (Sch 2, Form A):

"I, AB (designation) hereby undertake to pay to CD (designation) all sums due and that may become due by me to the said CD with interest from this date payable yearly; for which I grant a standard security in favour of the said CD over All and Whole [description of the security subjects]: The Standard Conditions specified in Schedule 3 to the Conveyancing and Feudal Reform (Scotland) Act 1970, and any lawful variation operative for the time being, shall apply: And I grant warrandice."

Of course, usually, a standard security is a more detailed document than simply this, but not necessarily much more detailed. It is usual for heritable creditors in the case of residential properties to use their own *pro forma* standard security and the solicitor merely has to complete the blanks.

Schedule 3: the Standard Conditions

To avoid a proliferation of lengthy documents all providing for a heritable creditor's own preferred obligations for the debtor to fulfil, the Act foresaw that such conditions could be provided for by the creation of a set of Standard Conditions which would, except where expressly amended, apply to all standard securities. The main purpose of the Standard Conditions is to impose upon the debtor certain provisions intended to maintain the value of the security subjects. For this reason the standard conditions contain obligations on the debtor to maintain and keep the subjects in repair, to make good any defects, to observe all title conditions imposed on the owner of the subjects, to pay any periodic payments due, to comply with any planning notices and orders issued, to keep the subjects insured to full market value (sometimes amended to full reinstatement value), not to let out the subjects or any part of them without the creditor's permission, and not to demolish alter or add to the buildings on the security subjects without the creditor's permission and without obtaining any necessary statutory consents. The standard conditions also give the creditor power to fulfil any of the debtor's obligations under the standard conditions and to charge the debtor any costs involved in so doing. But the purpose of the standard conditions is also wider than these protective obligations. They give a list of situations in which the debtor will be regarded as being in default and they detail certain of the rights of the creditor on default and on calling up the security. Given the broad range of conditions, it is no surprise that including a list of standard conditions considerably shortened the length of heritable security documents.

Enforcement

Another major feature of the reform was to provide for a simplified means of enforcing heritable securities in such a way as would be most equitable for both the creditor and debtor. Specifically, the evils created by court supervised enforced sales were swept away. It was well known (it is still a feature of some European systems of land law) that where enforcement action requires to be carried out by application to and supervision by a court, the procedures for adjudicating and taking possession of security subjects is very expensive. In addition when such a property is marketed, the fact that the property is being sold under duress is known to those viewing the property and offers for it are therefore likely to be considerably below the normal market price. Such evils are avoided by the system set up by the 1970 Act. The Act allows a creditor to take possession of security subjects without court involvement. In addition, the sale will not disclose the circumstances of the debtor's duress and so will be, to all intents and purposes, simply a normal market sale and will obtain the fair market value. That the procedures are fair is provided for by the requirement for proper advertisement and the obligation in s 25 of the Act that "it shall be a duty of the creditor to take all reasonable steps to ensure that the price at which all or any of the subjects are sold is the best that can be reasonably obtained". That the sale is being made by a heritable creditor will only be disclosed to the purchaser at the time of closing the missives and in the conveyancing. After such a sale the standard security simply "flies off", with no need for any court order. Thus the procedures are intended to obtain the best price that can be obtained in the circumstances. This gives the best prospects for repayment of the debt, minimises any shortfall, and maximises any net sum payable to the debtor after the debt has been paid off.

The precise procedures for carrying out an enforced sale involve three alternatives which have been criticised for being creditor-centred.

First, the creditor can serve a notice of default upon the debtor where there are circumstances in which the debtor is in default (s 21f) (see also Standard Condition 9 for the circumstances). The debtor has 1 month in which to purge the default. If he does not purge the default, then the creditor can enforce a sale. If the default is purged, then the debtor is effectively placed back in the situation in which he was prior to the notice. There should be no further consequences for the debtor. The normal situation giving rise to default is the failure by the debtor to pay a periodic instalment of loan and interest. A default notice should crystallise action by the debtor. Even if the debtor is unable to make the payment sought, the debtor might well be able to negotiate some other form of settlement which will cause the withdrawal of the default notice – for example, a payment holiday with the amount of the instalment added to the heritable debt, or alternatively a recalculation of the debt over a longer repayment period with consequentially reduced monthly payments. The notice of default is therefore flexible and can avoid the stigma and social consequences of an enforced sale. However, there is nothing to require a creditor to act with such a generous spirit and in practice many immediately adopt the second form of enforcement.

Second, a creditor can serve a calling-up notice requiring the debtor to repay the whole amount borrowed with interest within 2 months (s 19). Such a notice need not be preceded by any default – a creditor may simply wish to cease the debt. However, a creditor may be precluded from serving a calling-up notice because of other obligations undertaken with the debtor or because of the operation of law. But a calling-up notice immediately places a debtor in a difficult position and where the loan is over residential property this threatens to make the debtor homeless. Because of this it is now a requirement on the creditor in such circumstances to serve a notice upon the debtor's local authority advising them that the debtor is likely to be made homeless (s 19B, inserted in the 1970 Act by the Homelessness etc (Scotland) Act 2003, s 11). The use of the calling-up procedure instead of the somewhat fairer default procedure was held by some commentators to be oppressive and this led to the Mortgage Rights (Scotland) Act 2001 which was intended to fortify the debtor's rights.

Third, the creditor in circumstances in which the debtor is in default may apply to the court for a warrant to exercise any of the remedies open to a creditor on the debtor's default (a "s 24 warrant"). The usual reason for this procedure being used is where the proprietor of the security subjects is insolvent. Standard Condition 9 does not unambiguously specifically define what is meant by "insolvent" and there are circumstances in which, as a precaution, a creditor feels that it is necessary to have this formally established by the court lest the creditor's use of the remedies might subsequently be held to be oppressive or unwarranted.

Mortgage Rights (Scotland) Act 2001

In the case of all of these procedures, the debtor has the right to make objection to the court. But, in addition to that right, the debtor now has additional rights under the Mortgage Rights (Scotland) Act 2001. On application by the debtor, the court has the power to suspend the enforcement of a security "to the extent, period and subject to such conditions as it thinks ... reasonable in all the circumstances". But the court must consider four factors:

(1) the nature and reasons for the default;
(2) the applicant's ability to fulfil the default within a reasonable time;
(3) any action taken by a creditor to assist the debtor;
(4) the ability of the applicant and any other person residing in the security subjects to find reasonable alternative accommodation.

Additional advances

Another of the flexible features of a standard security is that the sum owed can be expressed in general terms covering both existing and also future advances by means of the expression "all sums due and that may become due". By means of this phrase, a creditor can make additional advances to the debtor and these additional advances will also be secured by the terms of the existing standard security. There are, however, some well-known problems associated with this generality.

Sometimes, a married couple or pair of civil partners, owning the residential security subjects in common, will enter into a joint and several loan secured over the property held in joint names. There is nothing essentially problematic about this, however, should one of the couple subsequently take out further loans from the same creditor, these further loans will also be secured and in this way the "innocent" partner will in a default situation have responsibility to make payment if the security is not to be sold. It is surprising how frequently in a matrimonial action such loans are discovered, with the "innocent" partner or spouse knowing absolutely nothing about them.

Another situation occurs when one of the partners, for perfectly proper business reasons (say, they are a partner in a firm) grants a personal guarantee for the firm's debts in favour of the creditor. This puts the security subjects at risk of being called up if the firm defaults on the debt it owes. Yet the "innocent" spouse or partner may know nothing of it. It also follows that even if the partners' own mortgage and overdraft is fully paid up, yet the creditor may still refuse to give a discharge of the standard security until the debt secured by the guarantee is also fully paid.

Nevertheless, the flexible phrase will operate to make the expenses and procedures of further advances cheap and simple – all that is generally required is a receipt for the money. So, if a debtor requires a further substantial loan to enable a roof repair to be carried out, this is simple to achieve provided that there is sufficient collateral to cover the additional advance.

Ranking

The alternative course of obtaining further sums is by means of a top-up loan from another creditor. This means that there are two standard securities and two loans to service.

In the event of a calling up, there may or may not be sufficient collateral value in the security subjects to enable the creditors both to be paid in full. What happens if there are insufficient funds to pay them both? The answer is that the securities "rank" and are paid in the order in which they appear on the registers. This accords with the maxim *prior tempore potior iure* (the earlier in time, the stronger the right). However, a creditor of the second charge could be put at a disadvantage in a winding-up if the first creditor makes subsequent additional advances. To remedy this possibility, s 13 of the Act provides that the second creditor can serve a notice of second charge on the first creditor. This restricts the amount of the first creditor's security to the present advances made (and any future advances which the first creditor is presently contracted to make) together with interest, present and future, and expenses and outlays.

Creditors can, and frequently for commercial purposes do, enter into ranking agreements between themselves. For example, in the purchase of a public house, the owner may obtain a commercial loan from a bank and at the same time a preferential interest loan from a brewery with, as one of its conditions, an obligation to purchase all or most of the liquid stock from the brewery at the wholesale prices operative from time to time. In these circumstances, the bank will insist in the prior charge and the brewery, knowing this, but anxious to ensure a continuing market for its products, will agree to have its standard security postponed to that of the bank. A ranking clause can easily be included in the brewery's standard security to this effect. It therefore will not matter in what order the standard securities appear on the registers, since the brewery loan will always remain postponed.

Flexibility – deeds of restriction and variation

A final flexible feature of the 1970 Act is that the statute provides for social and economic changes to take place over the life of a secured loan without the necessity of discharging the loan and creating a new one.

An assignation (s 14 and Forms A and B of Sch 4) allows a heritable creditor to transfer the secured loan to another party. The forms simply vest all rights and obligations of the former creditor in the second creditor from the date of the registration of the assignation. As from that date, the new creditor has the right to demand payment of capital and interest from the debtor, and also has the benefit of any notices served on the debtor and procedures instituted against the debtor.

A deed of restriction (s 15 and Forms C and D of Sch 4) allows a debtor to have a portion of the security subjects released from the security – usually on repayment of a substantial amount of the original loan. This is useful where, for example, a building company purchases a field for residential development and gives a standard security to its bank in security of a loan to cover development costs. At the time when developed plots are sold off to purchasers, the building company can obtain a deed of restriction for each plot, as it is sold. This means that the purchaser takes the plot free of any of the building company's debt. Of course, the area of the original security subjects will be reduced and it would be normal for the company to repay to its creditor a proportionate amount out of the proceeds of the sale of the plot. This provides a flexible way of securing the financing of the development.

A deed of variation (s 16 and Form F of Sch 4) allows a number of variations to be made, with the creditor's consent, to the debtor's original obligations. Most importantly a deed of variation can be used to release one of a number of original debtors from further liability, or to introduce a new debtor. Situations where this might be utilised occur where a single person, who owns their own property subject to a standard security, gets married and decides to make over a one-half share of the property to their partner who, in turn, agrees to undertake joint and several liability for the secured loan. Of course, the creditor will want to be sure of the new partner as a co-debtor before consenting to this change in the original obligation. Similarly, where a couple fall out and break up, one of them can take over the whole of the property and assume sole responsibility for the loan and the second can make over their share of the property to the first and be released from any further liability. Again, and perhaps more crucially this time, the creditor will want to ensure that the first partner is able to pay the capital and interest and fulfil the whole obligations under the standard security before consenting to the variation. In both cases, a suitably worded deed of variation can easily give effect to these changes in debtors.

INTERPLAY BETWEEN FIXED SECURITIES (INCLUDING STANDARD SECURITIES) AND FLOATING CHARGES

It will have been noticed that a number of the above securities are fixed securities (such as liens arising by operation of law over moveable property and standard securities granted over heritable security). These fixed securities create a real right in favour of the creditor from the time when the security is fixed. Floating charges, on the other hand, normally range over a company's whole assets (of whatever status, heritable or moveable) and may create viable forms of security over those assets, including fixed heritable assets of a company, only from the moment that the floating charges crystallise. There are therefore a number of problems about the interplay between the floating charges and fixed securities.

According to the Companies Act 2006, a crystallised floating charge is deemed to be subject to any preferential claims (Companies Act 1985, s 464), and so the effect of this is that a lien is always preferred to the floating charge. The 2006 Act provides that a standard security created and registered prior to crystallisation is in a similar preferential position. So it appears that a standard security, if registered or recorded prior to crystallisation, ranks prior to the floating charge. This means that the floating charge will attach to the balance of net funds after the heritable creditor has been paid. Clearly this places floating charge holders in a prejudiced position. Accordingly, it is usual for floating charges and standard securities to have ranking clauses stating that a floating charge will, upon crystallisation, rank prior to any fixed security registered or recorded on a later date than the floating charge.

However, the current law has recently been restated for Scotland by the Bankruptcy and Diligence etc (Scotland) Act 2007 (ss 37–49) which provides that floating charges will no longer be valid simply by being recorded in the charges section of the company's file held by Companies House. To give them validity it will be necessary for the floating charge to be registered in a new Register of Floating Charges to be kept by the Keeper of the Registers of Scotland (there is provision for a notice of a floating charge to be registered in the Register of Floating Charges and for the floating charge to have validity from the date of the notice provided that the charge itself is registered within 21 days of the notice). The new register is not expected to be in place until September 2009, and until the Register is operational the rules under the Companies Act 2006 remain in place.

Section 40 of the 2007 Act provides that standard securities and floating charges now rank in the order in which they were created (for a standard security this means the date when registered in the Land Register or Register of Sasines; for a floating charge this means the date when the charge (or the notice of the charge) was registered in the Register of Floating Charges, whichever is the earlier). Fixed securities arising by operation of law will continue to have priority over crystallised floating charges. The new law will therefore give a floating charge priority on crystallisation over a standard security, registered or recorded subsequently, and that without the need for a ranking agreement. However, the new legislation is flexible and allows a floating charge to contain a ranking agreement varying the statutory provisions as to ranking where these are agreed between the affected creditors.

DILIGENCES OVER HERITABLE PROPERTY

The Bankruptcy and Diligence etc (Scotland) Act 2007 when it comes into force will also sweep away existing forms of heritable diligence. By far the most common and useful form of heritable diligence is inhibition.

At present a person holding a court decree for payment of money can secure payment of the debt by obtaining letters of inhibition from the Court of Session (Rules of the Court of Session, Ch 59). Letters of inhibition, once registered in the Register of Inhibitions and Adjudications (which register is to be known as the Register of Inhibitions after the commencement of the Act), have the effect of preventing the debtor from selling, disponing, granting security over or burdening any of their heritable property for a period of 5 years. A schedule of inhibition is served upon the debtor and in the court's name forbids the debtor "from selling, disposing of, burdening or otherwise affecting your land and other heritable property to the prejudice of" the creditor. In addition, a person raising a court action for payment of money may in certain circumstances seek a warrant from the court for "inhibition on the dependence" of the action. In this way the pursuer can secure payment of the debt from the time of raising the action, long before the claim is proved. The pursuer does not therefore require to wait until decree has been obtained in the action before obtaining preferential status over the debtor's heritable assets. Inhibition on the dependence prevents a defender from denuding himself of his heritable property so as to defeat the pursuer's claim.

The 2007 Act also replaces adjudication (a little used method of forcing the sale of a debtor's heritable property) with a new form of diligence known as a "land attachment". Where a decree has been obtained against a debtor, and where a charge for payment has been made, and the debtor has not settled the debt during the time allowed, the pursuer may register a land attachment in the Register of Inhibitions. The land attachment has a similar effect to an inhibition in that the debtor is unable to sell, dispose, grant security or burden their land. After the land attachment has been in effect for at least 6 months and remains unpaid, the creditor can seek a warrant from the court to enforce a sale of the debtor's heritable property (s 92) and thus recover the debt. This power is not available where the debt is less than £3,000. Part 4 of the 2007 Act, which deals with land attachment, is not at the time of writing in force.

Essential Facts

- **Stages in transfer of moveable and heritable property:** there are three stages in the transfer of property which allow the giving of security: contract (*consensus*); assignation (which creates personal rights); and delivery (which creates real rights). Delivery is generally essential for the creation of security but there are exceptions.

- **Rights in security:** To secure the payment of money and other obligations undertaken by an owner of property, it is common to secure these using the debtor's property. This enables the creditor to take possession of the property if the debtor fails to fulfil his obligations. This is usually achieved by *delivery* of the property by the debtor to the creditor. But delivery can be actual, constructive or merely symbolical according to the type of property concerned. The best-known examples of security by delivery over moveable property are *pledge* and *lien*. Security over heritable property is achieved by the debtor registering or recording a *standard security* in favour of the creditor. An exception to the general requirement for delivery exists with floating charged and with *hypothecs*.

- **Floating charges:** these are a form of security without delivery. A company can grant a floating charge over its whole undertaking (being over its whole assets, moveable and heritable). The floating charge must be registered in the Companies file (and in the Register of Floating Charges). In the event of default, a floating charge crystallises and a real right is created in favour of the creditor over the assets.

- **Hypothecs:** these are a form of security without formal delivery. Conventional hypothecs arise out of contract and are usually maritime, allowing the master of a ship to raise funds in an emergency. There are also certain legal hypothecs such as those in favour of a solicitor or landlord.

- **Pledge:** this exists where moveable property is delivered to a creditor in security of the debtor's obligation for repayment. Delivery is usually by actual physical transfer, but in some circumstances, may be constructive or symbolical. Pledges are a very important form of commercial security.

- **Lien:** these are forms of security implied by law where a person holding the property of another has legal rights over that property in security of obligations owed to them by the debtor. Liens may be special (restricted to the transaction giving rise to the creditor's possession of the property and the debtor's obligation to pay money relating to the transaction) or general (available over any of the debtor's property held by the creditor and may be used in security for any balances of money owed over a course of dealing involving a number of transactions between the debtor and creditor). Common forms of lien are those of a factor, banker, solicitor and innkeeper.

- **Standard securities:** the Conveyancing and Feudal Reform (Scotland) Act 1970 abolished older forms of heritable security and replaced them with one simple and flexible form: the standard security. There are statutory standard conditions which oblige the debtor to maintain the capital value of the security subjects. As a result, the debtor is obliged to maintain and keep the subjects in repair, to make good any defects, to observe all title conditions imposed on the owner of the subjects, to pay any periodic payments due, to comply with any planning notices and orders issued, to keep the subjects insured to full market value (sometimes amended to full reinstatement value), not to let the subjects or any part of them without the creditor's permission, and not to demolish alter or add to the buildings on the security subjects without the creditor's permission and without obtaining any necessary statutory consents. The standard conditions also give the creditor power to fulfil the debtor's obligation and they state certain of the debtor's rights on default. The 1970 Act also provides three means of enforcement in the event of the debtor's breach of his obligations: (1) default procedure (where the debtor has one month to put right the default, which failing the property can be sold by the creditor); (2) calling-up procedure (whereby the debtor must repay the whole loan within 2 months (which failing the property can be sold by the creditor)); and (3) s 24 warrant (where in certain circumstances the creditor can go to the court (to obtain enforcement powers)).

- **Deed of variation:** a deed of variation is a document between the debtor and heritable creditor (and third party) which brings into effect a variation of the obligations undertaken by the debtor. Often this is used to enable one of two or more debtors to be released, or to enable a third party to be introduced as a co-debtor along with the original debtor. The deed of variation is therefore an important document where there are changes in matrimonial status of debtors.

- **Deed of restriction:** a deed of restriction is a deed granted by a heritable creditor allowing the release of part of the secured subjects – usually on payment of a sum of money to the creditor in part repayment of the loan. Deeds of restriction are very important in conveyancing practice as they allow a builder who is developing an estate to borrow money over the estate and yet to have completed plots released from the security so that they may be sold to purchasers.

- **Interplay between fixed securities (including standard securities) and floating charges:** a lien always has priority over a floating charge. However, under the Companies Act 2006, a standard security, if registered or recorded prior to crystallisation, ranks prior to the floating charge. This means that the floating charge will only attach to the balance of net funds after the heritable creditor has been paid. The position is likely to be radically altered when the Bankruptcy and Diligence etc (Scotland) Act 2007 comes into force. The 2007 Act requires new floating charges to be registered in a new register: the Register of Floating Charges. Such floating charges and standard securities will thereafter rank in the order in which they were registered regardless of the date of any crystallisation. It will remain the position that floating charges can contain ranking clauses varying the statutory provisions as to ranking where these have been agreed among the affected creditors.

- **Diligences over heritable property:** under the current law, a creditor holding a decree against a debtor can obtain letters of inhibition which have the effect of preventing a debtor from selling, disponing, granting security over or burdening any of their heritable property for a period of 5 years. Inhibition can also be granted on the dependence of a court action thus instantly inhibiting the defender's heritable property pending the outcome of the court action. The Bankruptcy and Diligence etc (Scotland) Act 2007 will replace the inhibition with a new form of land attachment which is similar but has the added advantage for the creditor that, after the land attachment has been in effect for 6 months and the debt remains unpaid, the creditor can enforce the sale of the debtor's property (provided the debt exceeds £3,000).

4 HERITABLE PROPERTY: LAND OWNERSHIP

HISTORY OF LAND TENURE – FEUDAL TENURE

The origins of Scottish land tenure are obscured by the mists of time, but it is known that around the 13th century the feudal system was introduced into the kingdom of Scotland having steadily worked its influence north through England following the Norman Conquest.

Feudalism was a political system of control in which the king was regarded as the original and ultimate owner of the land. The king surrounded himself with powerful nobles whom, in exchange for their pledge of allegiance ("fealty"), he would reward with grants of land. The king continued to have an interest in the land and was entitled to look to the nobles for military and financial support. It follows that there then existed two layers of ownership: the interest of the king as ultimate feudal superior, and the interest of the favoured noble as vassal. In their turn, such nobles were able to make further feudal grants of portions of their new land to their own supporters, and so on *ad infinitum* (this process of being able to make a further feudal grant of land to a new vassal is called "subinfeudation").

At each level of feudal grant the relationship was one of superior and vassal, and the superior always a retained an interest to receive military or other services from the new vassal. The vassal at the lowest level was the person who occupied the land and had the right to work the land and enjoy its fruits. The interest of the occupying vassal is known in the law as the *dominium utile* (the right to use the land and enjoy the fruits of the land) while the interest of the superiors is referred to as the *dominium directum*.

It follows that in a feudal system of land holding there therefore existed a hierarchy of interests in land with the king at the apex as ultimate superior, with the occupying vassal at the lowest level, and with one or more mid-superiors.

The great advantage of the feudal system was that it effectively subordinated a large number of otherwise politically powerful individuals while, at the same time as disempowering them, giving vassals an interest in retaining the political system and good reasons to recognise the authority of the superiors and of the king as ultimate superior. At a stroke, feudal systems introduced an enviable level of political stability. They also ensured a continuing line of income for superiors.

Until the 18th century, the noble landowners, who were immediate vassals of the king, held what were known as barony titles and these barons held rights to hold a baron's court where the king's law would be imposed, with the baron sitting in judgment. Such jurisdictions were considered a political threat at the time of the Jacobite uprisings and were finally abolished in 1746. In 1745, the right of a superior to demand military service ("ward holding") from the vassal was also abolished.

By 1746, the influence of political feudalism had therefore waned and in effect the system of landholding in Scotland thereafter was in legal terms little more than a form of real contracts, though incorporating the language of feudalism. As a result, if an owner of property wished to sell the property and impose obligations in perpetuity on a purchaser as proprietor of the land being sold, it was normal to grant a feu disposition to the purchaser and incorporate the conditions as burdens affecting the lands. In the feu disposition, the seller would be referred to as the "superior" and the purchaser as the "vassal". The feu disposition recorded that the superior retained an interest in the land (a "*reddendo*") which most frequently amounted to the payment of a fixed sum of money paid yearly (a "feuduty"). More than likely, the superior was paying a feuduty to his own superior. In addition to receiving an annual feuduty, superiors could charge an additional payment of feuduty when one vassal sold out and was replaced by a new vassal. Such entry payments were termed a "casualty" and continued on the entry of each new vassal until about 1914 when they were finally abolished (Feudal Casualties (Scotland) Act 1914).

The imposed feudal conditions could be enforced by the superior but not by anyone else (unless the superior included such a right within the terms of the condition. Such a right to allow a third party to enforce the condition was known as a "*ius quaesitum tertio*" and was uncommon). In the event of breach, the superior could even *irritate* the feu and recover possession from the vassal. If the vassal found the feudal conditions were too onerous or prevented him from carrying out some form of desired enjoyment, the vassal could ask the superior for a waiver of the condition and this was often granted on the payment of compensation (the amount being fixed by the superior). In these ways, the superior retained real and enforceable interests in the land owned by the vassal. For many people, the possibility of such forms of economic exploitation by superiors with no other connection with a locality, was regarded as unacceptable and this feeling reached its height at the time of the Wilson Labour Government of 1964 which commenced the process of feudal abolition. There is no doubt that, prior to abolition of feudal tenure, some individuals regarded the collection of superiorities as a means of financial investment. While feuduty collection in later years became an ever more expensive aspect of superiority, the promise of the occasional lump sum obtained in consideration for a minute of waiver of a condition was more tempting. Effectively the superior set the price for such waivers and by setting too high a price could prevent property within the superiority from being developed. One of the first reforms after the commencement of the process of abolition enabled a vassal to redeem their feuduty (paying a lump sum to the superior to end the annual payment of feuduty) at a figure of around 12 times the annual feuduty payable (after 1974 an allocated feuduty was required to be redeemed at the time of the sale of a property).

THE ABOLITION OF FEUDAL TENURE

The process of abolition was commenced by the publishing of a number of White Papers and other reports.

One of the first reforming Acts was the Conveyancing and Feudal Reform (Scotland) Act 1970 which, apart from providing for standard securities, allowed a vassal to apply to the Lands Tribunal for Scotland as an alternative means of having an onerous feudal condition waived. The Tribunal would determine a reasonable compensation (Conveyancing and Feudal Reform (Scotland) Act 1970, s 1).

The Land Tenure Reform (Scotland) Act 1974 reformed the law relating to feuduties and provided a vassal with a means of redeeming a feuduty allocated on the *dominium utile* and, in addition, provided for the compulsory redemption of allocated feuduties on the occurrence of a sale of the property.

After the enactment of the 1970 and 1974 Acts, some practitioners felt that the process of feudal reform had gone far enough, and certainly reform appeared to stagnate for a very extended period of years until feudal tenure was finally abolished by the Abolition of Feudal Tenure etc (Scotland) Act 2000, s 1 of which makes the stark statement that "The feudal system of land tenure, that is to say the entire system whereby land is held by a vassal on perpetual tenure from a superior is, on the appointed day, abolished". The appointed day was Sunday, 28 November 2004. From the appointed day, land in Scotland is no longer held on feudal tenure, but rather is held "allodially" (owned outright and under no superior). Allodial land was known to the law of Scotland previously in the form of certain forms of Church property, the "udal" lands of Orkney and Shetland, and land which had been acquired through statutory compulsory purchase. These were all held free of the interest of any superior. Now, however, allodial land holding is universal across Scotland.

Since the appointed day, the most striking feature of reform has been the loss of the language of feudalism. Conditions of land tenure have not disappeared, as some thought would happen. It is the right of a feudal superior to enforce conditions as superior alone that has disappeared. Conditions that are purely feudal have become obsolete, and conditions are now to be understood as a legal relationship existing between two properties: a burdened property which must suffer the effect of the condition on the one hand, and a benefited property which has the benefit of the condition on the other hand (see below).

At the same time as carrying out the process of reforming and later abolishing feudal tenure, another separate reforming process was introduced by statute, namely that of the replacement of the Register of Sasines (the register of documents of title to land) with the Land Register (a register of state-guaranteed titles to land organised around a system of map-based land descriptions). We will examine some of the implications of this reform in Chapter 5. This reform was achieved by the Land Registration (Scotland) Act 1979.

As a result of these two quite separate processes of reform, the nature of land tenure conveyancing in Scotland has changed markedly over the last 40 years. We shall examine some aspects of conveyancing in Chapter 5. What is remarkable is that in many respects there has remained a significant continuity in land law. This is no doubt due to the fact that the practical influence of feudalism was already at a relatively low level even when the reforming process began, while the importance of Roman law in forming the common law of land ownership in Scotland was much more influential – even though not so prominent in the consciousness of many practitioners. We must now turn to this common law.

NATURAL RIGHTS IN PROPERTY – SUPPORT

We saw in Chapter 1 that property is "the right of using or disposing of a subject as our own, except in so far as we are restrained by law or paction" (Erskine). Landownership is similarly constrained. Natural rights are those rights which are necessary for the normal enjoyment of property and which arise by way of the operation of the common law. There are generally recognised to be three sorts: support, rights in water and rights to enjoy property without nuisance. The last two types of natural rights we shall examine below. First we shall consider the right of support, minerals rights and common law rights ancillary to salmon fishing rights.

Right of support

An owner of land is entitled to expect that the surface of the land will not subside. It follows that the proprietor of adjoining land must not cut away earth or rock which provides support for the surface of the neighbouring land and which excavations are likely to lead to the subsidence of the surface of the neighbouring land.

Strictly, the right of support is not a positive obligation and the owner of land is under a duty only to refrain from doing acts which might jeopardise the neighbouring land as it exists in its natural state. The courts may not uphold a corresponding duty to provide support for neighbouring land loaded with heavy buildings.

Right of support is also an important aspect of the "law of the tenement" which we shall explain in Chapter 5, for the owner of a tenement flat is entitled to the support of his flat by the foundations and walls below (s 8(1) of the Tenements (Scotland) Act 2004).

Minerals – and their relevance to rights of support

In mining areas an owner of land may sever the mineral rights and make these over to a mining company as a separate interest in land. In this way the minerals can be economically exploited but the interest of the owner of the surface should not be affected given that the owner of the surface is entitled to a common law right of support. To achieve separation of minerals, the owner of a larger area of ground may sell off plots of ground to purchasers subject to a "reservation of minerals" (that is, keeping the minerals in the ownership of the seller). This is usually achieved by means of a burden incorporated in the purchaser's title deeds. Unfortunately, where mining operations have been undertaken it is not uncommon for the surface to subside. Generally speaking, a reservation of minerals is not a problem for a title in a built-up residential area provided that it is subject to restrictions preventing surface entry (ie by means of mine shafts) and giving compensation for any subsidence which underground workings might cause.

The right of support is not a positive obligation on the owner of the minerals, but is negative in that the owner of the minerals must avoid acts interfering with the *existing* support – ie must not do acts which do or are likely to interfere with the load-bearing characteristics of the surface. The emphasis on "existing support", of course, means that if the owner of the surface has a title subject to a reservation of minerals and then develops the surface by putting loads on it which are new and heavy then there is no breach of duty if the increased load causes the surface to subside. Similar provisions occur if water is re-routed or retained on the surface such that the load of water threatens load bearing or that the load-bearing structure of the surface is changed by new water penetration into the subsoil and rock. Other than this negative obligation, the owner of the minerals is entitled to continue working the minerals. If the owner of the surface has objective reasons to think that mining is likely to cause subsidence then they have the remedy of interdict. Where there is subsidence or surface damage the remedy is payment of monetary damages.

It is therefore common for a purchaser in an area where mineral workings are known, to require a specialist report on the minerals to assess whether the land is one where valuable minerals occur, or where workings have been carried out historically, and hence whether there is any known threat of subsidence.

Any provision for compensation against a mining company is often less than useful when relying only on the common law provisions (some coal mines are hundreds of years old and finding exactly where they are and who is responsible under common law can be impossible). Apart from the common law, there are some statutory compensation schemes such as that offered by the Coal Authority (see the Coal Mining Subsidence Act 1991, as amended by the Coal Industry Act 1994).

Common law rights ancillary to salmon fishing

A grant of salmon fishing rights is a separate and severable interest in land from the rights of the land ownership. It is common for salmon fishing rights in non-tidal rivers to be included in the rights of the owners of the shore (where the title deeds grant the rights *cum piscationibus salmonum*) and they are implied in a grant of a barony. However, such rights may be sold as a separate estate and this is not infrequent when the rights are granted over the foreshore (the area of the seashore covered by high tide and exposed by the low tide). It follows from such a grant that the owner of the salmon fishings is given natural rights at common law to enjoy those fishings. The ancillary rights include a right of access over the property of adjoining proprietors, the right to draw up and moor boats, and the right to clean, dry and repair nets on adjoining ground. In each case the common law rights must be exercised only as is necessary for the normal enjoyment of the fishing rights and in a manner least prejudicial to the neighbouring proprietors concerned. However, the rights are real rights and can be enforced in the courts against the adjacent proprietors if they are resisted.

Such rights still exist but have become less and less important as the salmon fisheries have declined. They are frequently overlooked.

WATER RIGHTS

Water in rivers, streams and other definite channels

Rain falling over the land rises to the surface at springs and flows from them along streams and rivers until reaching the sea. These streams and rivers have definite channels albeit at various scales and it is therefore necessary to consider whether water can be owned and who may use it. Roman law provides the key to these issues. The water flowing in these channels is not owned but all the proprietors of the land through which the water flows on its path to the sea (the "riparian proprietors") have a common interest in the flowing water and so are entitled to make use of the water for ordinary domestic purposes such as the quenching of thirst of humans and animals, and for the purposes of washing and cooking. Water may not be taken liberally for all purposes, however. In the case of industrial and agricultural purposes which consume large quantities of water (such as industry or irrigation), the riparian proprietors may take as much water as they need but on the proviso that there is sufficient water remaining in the channel to provide for the common interest of the lower riparian proprietors' ordinary domestic uses. In addition the water left running in the channels should not be reduced in quality by extraction or non-domestic purposes. This common law requirement to maintain an appropriate quality of flowing water is now added to by a number of statutory provisions.

Who owns the channel through which the water flows? This question is answered by Roman law which holds that the riparian proprietors on either side of the channel have right to the land up to the mid point in the channel (the "*medium filum*").

We have seen in Chapter 1, how the effects of *alluvio* (gradual erosion and deposition of soil causing a slow movement of river courses over time) and *avulsio* (flood waters) may have effects on boundaries of land bordered by a river.

However, where a river flows through a piece of land which is in sole ownership, the proprietor may change the course of the river as he pleases, provided that by the time the edge of the owner's property is reached the flow has been returned to its original course as it exits the land.

Water in lochs

Water in lochs which exist wholly within the land of one proprietor are the property of that proprietor who has complete control over the water and can use it as he wishes – save only for that fact that he must have regard for the common interest of any proprietors served by a stream or outflow originating in the loch and flowing through the land of lower riparian proprietors.

Where a loch is on land owned by a number of adjoining proprietors, it may be used by any and all of the proprietors as they have a joint right in the water. Each proprietor is presumed to own the *solum* (ground under the loch) adjacent to his land extending as far as the middle of the loch. This presumption may be qualified by titles or title deeds which make alternative provision.

Water in the sea

Water in the sea and in tidal rivers is not capable of being owned by adjacent proprietors.

REGALIA

Roman law provided that certain rights in land were held by the community for the benefit of all persons. In the Roman Empire such community items included sporting arenas and temples, but the principles of Roman law have been adapted to deal with Scottish society and so community property in our society involves the sea, foreshore, salmon fishings and precious metals which are regarded in law as being held by the Crown in trust for the public. The name for such property is *"regalia"* and there are two classes: *regalia majora* (property held by the Crown in trust for the public which cannot be alienated and made over for individuals to possess) and *regalia minora* (property held by the Crown which can be made over for individuals to possess).

Regalia majora

These include:

(1) the sea within United Kingdom territorial waters which is held in trust for the public purposes of navigation and fishing;

(2) the foreshore (the area of the seashore covered by high tide and exposed by the low tide) which is again held in trust for navigation and fishing and also for public recreation; and

(3) tidal rivers again for the purposes of navigation and fishing.

Regalia minora

These include:

(1) the *precious metals* of gold, silver and high-grade lead. The Crown will alienate the title to work and win these on payment to the Crown of a royalty – a fee levied at a rate which relates to the amount worked and won from the ground;

(2) *salmon fishings*, which as we have seen above can be alienated either to the owner of the adjacent land or to another person and which include common law rights of access, mooring, and net hanging; and

(3) *foreshore* which can be alienated to the owner of the adjacent land or to any other person for the purposes of taking materials and collecting seaweed (at one time a valuable source of minerals and so used for the extraction of those minerals or as a natural manure). In this case, the new owner of the foreshore must have regard for the interests of the public for navigation, fishing and recreation. Scotland has a long tradition of recognising the natural right of the public to roam freely over the countryside and not merely the foreshore. It was once said that there was no law of trespass in Scotland. In addition, public rights of way have long been acknowledged (a public right of way exists where a road between and connecting two public places is used by the public frequently and over a period of 20 years). The right to roam over the countryside is now statutorily provided for in the Land Reform (Scotland) Act 2003.

NUISANCE

Another natural right of ownership of land is the right to be able to enjoy the property without having to suffer nuisance or disturbance caused by the proprietors of neighbouring property.

What amounts to a nuisance is a matter of fact and degree and depends on the established uses of property in the locality. For example, in a residential area, the sounds of normal domestic purposes (noises of walking on floors, running up and down stairs, conversation and even the flushing of lavatories) are to be regarded as normal and thus do not constitute a nuisance. Nuisances are disturbances which are out of character for the locality concerned.

In addition, the degree of disturbance is also to be considered. It was established in the case of *Watt* v *Jamieson* (1954) that disturbance must be more than can be borne by a reasonable man or woman ("*plus quam tolerabile*"). A sufferer can petition the court for interdict to force the person causing the nuisance to desist from doing so. However, if a nuisance has persisted for a lengthy period prior to objection, the complainer's right to object can be lost by prescription. For example, a neighbour cannot object to the noise and smells coming from a bakery which has been trading in a locality without objection for a period of over 20 years.

BURDENS AND SERVITUDES

Burdens and servitudes are different types of title conditions restricting the uses of land. They are frequently confused but actually have very different natures.

Burdens are conditions which are imposed contractually (originally feudally) when it is desired to create obligations to be suffered by the proprietor of a burdened property and which benefits the proprietor of a benefited property. For example, at the time of developing a block of flats, the developer can burden each property with a share of the expenses of maintenance, repair and renewal as necessary of common areas serving all the proprietors. Such a burden regulates the rights and obligations of the purchasers of properties on the estate and are therefore for the general benefit of all the owners. In this example, each flat will be burdened by having to pay its own share of the common expenses, but each flat will also be a benefited property in that the owner can in turn force the other proprietors to pay their shares. It is generally a matter of choice for the developer whether and how to impose such burdens. The imposition of such burdens is a major way in which to maintain a satisfactory level of amenity in an estate. To be effective, burdens must be expressed in writing and will appear in the titles of both the burdened and benefited properties.

Servitudes, on the other hand, are not a matter of choice but a matter of law. A servitude is a condition which provides a benefit to the proprietor of a piece of ground which is necessary to enable the proprietor of the benefited property to have normal enjoyment of the land. For example, a servitude right of access to a benefited property over adjoining property will be a necessary prerequisite to the enjoyment of the benefited land. Without it the land could not be reached at all and enjoyment would be impossible. Originally there was a fixed class of types of servitude divided into rural and urban types. This is no longer the case. Servitudes are often expressly stated in writing and so will appear in the titles of both benefited and burdened properties, but they also may arise by implication, by necessity, or by use without objection over a 20-year prescriptive period. When they are not express, they are overriding interests which will not generally appear in the Land Register.

Burdens

With the abolition of the feudal system of land holding, feudal conditions (at least to the extent that they are enforceable by feudal superiors) are abolished. But real burdens continue to exist provided that there is always a benefited property (otherwise sometimes known (especially when we are talking about servitudes) as a dominant tenement) and a burdened property (a servient tenement). The governing law is the Title Conditions (Scotland) Act 2003. Real burdens are now of two types: (1) affirmative burdens (which are obligations to do something – such as to maintain a boundary) and (2) negative burdens (which are obligations not to do something – such as not to build a house on the land).

When a property is transferred to the Land Register on a first registration (see Chapter 5), the Keeper will simply copy the wording of the previous burdens from the existing Sasine deeds. The Keeper will state what deed the original burden is in and then narrate the wording of the burden in full. (Servitudes do not appear on the GRS unless constituted in a written deed. The Keeper will not note servitudes created by implication or prescription. Such servitudes are regarded as "overriding interests").

Creation of real burdens

Even though feudal tenure has been abolished, real burdens can still be created, usually only in two circumstances: (1) when land is subdivided; or (2) when land is developed. To have legal effect the real burdens when created now have to be entered into the deeds (General Register of Sasines) or title sheets (Land Register) of both the affected properties. This was not the case prior to 28 November 2004 – before which date it was only necessary that the burden be recorded in the deeds of the servient tenement.

Subdivision of a piece of ground

In this situation a piece of ground is sold off and it is envisaged that it shall be used for a particular purpose. For example, if a house is to be built on the land, then the purchaser of the house needs to have necessary rights of access, water supply pipes, sewerage pipes, power lines and other services. The seller, the owner of the larger piece of ground of which the piece of ground being sold forms part, may want to ensure that the new land will have only one house on it, will only be used for domestic and not for commercial purposes and that it will be built to a height so that it does not interfere with the sellers existing view and does not put the seller's existing property into shadow (that is that it does not interfere with the sellers "rights of light and prospect"). Both purchaser and seller will want to ensure that there are reasonable obligations to enclose the new land with appropriate boundaries and that these should be maintained in future on some equitable basis. Such burdens will need to be expressed in full in the disposition conveying the smaller piece of ground to the purchaser. On registering the purchaser's title, the burdens become real conditions which are enforceable by the seller and his successors in title to the larger piece of ground against the purchaser and his successors in title to the smaller piece of ground. The burdens are in this way burdens of tenure of the smaller piece of ground.

A conveyancer should ensure that the terms of any real burdens that it is intended to enforce, will have been agreed in advance in the missives (see Chapter 5 for the purpose and contents of missives).

Development case

In this case, a builder developing an estate will intend to split the larger piece of ground into a number of individual plots on which houses or flats are to be built. To achieve this, the builder will want to register or record a deed of conditions which will include burdens regulating the common and amenity areas, facilities and roads, and stating conditions about the maintenance and repair of these common areas, facilities and roads, and of the apportionment of the costs of such maintenance and repair among all the properties to be completed on the developed estate. The builder will also include additional burdens regulating the uses of the individual plots such as are necessary to ensure the amenity of the development and for the benefit of the owners of the individual plots as a whole. The deed of conditions (which usually includes a plan to show the layout of the estate and the position of its plots and common and amenity areas and roads) will merely be of the form of a memorandum and does not convey any property.

The conveyance of the individual plots to the purchasers is achieved by dispositions to individual purchasers. These dispositions will sell the flat or house and any land pertaining to it together with proportionate *pro indiviso* share of the common areas. The disposition will also refer to the deed of conditions for the burdens to the property as containing the conditions of tenure.

Once all the plots have been sold off, the builder will typically retain no rights of property at all in the plot. The deed of conditions then becomes enforceable by the whole owners of the estate against each other. Maintenance of common and amenity areas will typically be done through a residents' association who may employ a factor to do work for it and to send out bills to the individual owners with the costs apportioned on the basis stated in the deed of conditions. Roads on the estate will continue to be the responsibility of the whole owners of the estate until these are taken over by a local authority for maintenance. It is common for a builder to obtain a roads bond – a form of insurance policy – as a guarantee that the roads on the estate will be finally made up to the standard required by the local authority as a prerequisite for being taken over.

Real burdens and planning law compared and contrasted

Some have argued that title conditions are unnecessary as conditions of development can be imposed by planning authorities as part of the original planning permission. Such planning conditions are enforceable only by the planning authority and cannot be enforced by residents of an estate. A planning authority must act in the interest of the residents in the whole planning area and not act merely on behalf of the residents of an individual estate no matter how upset those residents may be. As a result, planning authorities may not be concerned with certain forms of minor infringement while the residents may be greatly offended by infringements which directly affect the perceived amenity of the estate. Frequently planners will not take action when planning conditions are infringed in a minor way. It is also not unknown for planning authorities to change their mind about conditions in later planning applications and grant planning consents with conditions different from those formerly thought appropriate to an area.

As a result, title conditions provide a more consistent basis for ensuring that the amenity of an individual locality is preserved. For example, a planning authority may grant a hotel licence to a formerly domestic property, while an appropriately worded title condition could be used to prevent the property from being operated as a licensed business.

The permissible content of a real burden

A burden is referred to as "praedial", which means that it must confer a real benefit on the benefited property. In the case of *Marsden* v *Craighelen*

Lawn Tennis and Squash Club (1999), there was a real burden which prohibited the playing of tennis on a Sunday. The question for the court was whether the burden was intended to preserve the tranquillity of the Sabbath day or whether the original superior simply had strong religious views and did not like frivolous games on the Sabbath. The former interpretation was praedial and affected the continuing enjoyment of the benefited property and so was praedial, while the latter interpretation was intended only to benefit the superior as an individual and so was not praedial – not benefiting the enjoyment of the land.

In addition to conferring a real benefit, a burden must not be contrary to public policy, must not impose a periodical payment (for example, like a feuduty), nor may it be repugnant to ownership (it must not prevent the owner of the burdened property having the normal rights of enjoyment of property (the burden must not prevent the owner from doing any of the usual juridical acts of sale, secured borrowing and the like), nor may a burden create a monopoly.

A real burden may include a right of pre-emption (effectively an option in favour of the dominant owner to purchase back the burdened property at the most favourable terms offered on the occasion of the exposure for sale of the burdened property (a pre-emption may be accepted or refused on one occasion only) but it may not include a right of redemption (which would entitle the owner of the dominant tenement to acquire the servient tenement on specified terms or at a specified time of his own controlling).

The wording of a real burden

Only an owner can burden his property. The terms of the burden have to appear in the deeds of both burdened and benefited properties. The burden must therefore identify both. This can be problematic with burdens created prior to 28 November 2004 and special rules have been developed to assist in this situation.

The wording of a burden must also specify adequately the terms of the burden. The wording of both burdens and express servitudes is interpreted strictly by the courts. There is a presumption for freedom. Accordingly the words are given the narrowest possible meaning. For example, an obligation to build a house of a particular type does not prevent the building of an additional house or houses of another type; an obligation to supply water does not necessitate that the water is of drinkable quality; an obligation to build a house and a garage does not prevent the building of a second garage; an obligation not to use a house for commercial purposes does not prevent part of it from being so used provided that the main purpose remains residential; and so on.

The wording of a burden has to stand on its own and must therefore not refer to something outside the deed which constitutes it. As a result in the case of *Aberdeen Varieties Ltd* v *James F Donald (Aberdeen Cinemas) Ltd* (1939), a burden was declared invalid since it referred to an Act of Parliament and could not be understood on its own in the absence of the Act. On the other hand, obligations to maintain a property where it is stated that the costs will be apportioned on the basis of rateable value, feuduty or some other specified basis will not be invalid even if the value or feuduty is not specified in the constituting deed but is specified in a public register or elsewhere.

Real burdens are only enforceable once they have appeared in the recorded or registered titles of all affected properties (the burdened and benefited properties). Conditions specified in deeds of conditions are enforceable by and against parties whose titles to their respective plots have been registered as soon as they are so registered.

Division of benefited and burdened properties

Division of burdened properties makes no difference as all the plots so formed will continue to be burdened. Where a benefited property is divided this could give rise to a proliferation of enforcement rights. The 2003 Act provides that unless the dispositions which divide the benefited property provide that they are all benefited, then any split-off will immediately cease to be a benefited property.

Personal burdens

The 2003 Act provides for certain types of personal burden. This means a burden which is held by a person without reference to any benefited property. Only two types need be mentioned: (1) conservation burdens where the public interest in the protection of the natural or built environment may be enforced by the Scottish Ministers, local authorities or certain designated conservation bodies; and (2) an economic development burden where the public interest is the promotion of economic development – a rather unspecific notion – which may be enforced by the Scottish Ministers or local authorities.

Extinction of real burdens

This can be achieved by four means:

(1) by *minute of waiver*: where all parties involved (and the whole benefited properties must be identified) agree to remove or restrict the operation of a real burden. For the amendment of community burdens it is sufficient if the majority of the identified benefited owners in the estate or their management agent sign or signs the waiver;

(2) by *Lands Tribunal application* by the owner of the burdened property: an application may be made to the tribunal and served on all interested parties. The tribunal has statutory power to waive or vary conditions (see Pt 9 of the 2003 Act);

(3) by *negative prescription and acquiescence*: after 5 years a material breach of a real burden can extinguish it by negative prescription (s 18 of the 2003 Act: formerly the negative prescriptive period was 20 years). The burden is extinguished by acquiescence if the owners of the benefited property or properties have consented to the breach, or if work carried out by the burdened proprietor renders the enforcement of the burden impossible as specified in the burden, and the benefited proprietor(s) knew or ought reasonably to have known about the work and yet did nothing to object or enforce their interest over the negative prescriptive period. Such burdens are only removed by negative prescription and acquiescence in so far as they have been breached.

(4) by the operation of the "*sunset rule*" which is intended to enable obsolete burdens to be removed: where a burden is over a hundred years old the owner of the burdened property can draw up a notice of termination. This has to be served on the owners of all the benefited properties and publicised by attachment of a copy of the notice to burdened properties and nearby lamp-posts. The burden will cease unless objection is made to the Lands Tribunal within 8 weeks by a benefited party who wishes the burden to remain.

Servitudes

The only servitudes now recognised as such are "positive servitudes" (which allow the owner of the dominant tenement to do something over the land of the servient tenement) – as opposed to a "negative servitude" (which formerly obliged a servient tenement owner not to do something) and which have been re-classified as forms of real burden.

Creation of servitudes

Servitudes can be created by:

(1) *express deed*: the deed of servitude is granted by the owner of the servient tenement and the deed is registered or recorded against the titles of both servient and dominant tenements;

(2) *use followed by positive prescription*: here, the owner of the dominant tenement exercises the acts constituting the servitude openly and without objection for the prescriptive period of 20 years. The acts constituting the servitude must be such that it can be said unambiguously that a legal right was being asserted. That is to say, that acts must not be exercised in secret, nor can acts allowed merely by way of a personal permission granted to the owner of the dominant tenement ripen into a servitude. At the end of the 20-year prescriptive period, acts carried out as a right, openly and without objection, will ripen into a servitude enforceable by the owner of the dominant tenement against the owner of the servient tenement;

(3) *implication and necessity*: where the owner of a piece of ground sells off a part of that ground in favour of a purchaser, then such rights as are omitted from express statement in the disposition in favour of the purchaser, but which are absolutely or reasonably necessary to allow the seller to enjoy their property, will be implied. The leading case is that of *Bowers* v *Kennedy* (2000). This case involved a piece of land which was divided into two separate properties, one wholly enclosed within the other. At the outset the only way to access the enclosed piece of ground was by way of a road through the larger piece of ground. There came a time when the enclosed piece of ground ceased to be used for an extended period in excess of 20 years. When the owners of the enclosed piece of ground started to access it again, the owner of the larger piece of ground objected on the basis that the servitude right of access had ceased to exist as a result of non-use over the negative prescriptive period of 20 years (with servitudes, rights can be both acquired and lost if exercised/not exercised for the 20-year period). The effect of the loss of the access meant that the enclosed piece of ground had become landlocked. In the particular circumstances of *Bowers*, the court held that since the servitude right of access was absolutely necessary for the enjoyment of the enclosed piece of ground, then there must always exist an implied right of access due to necessity and that this implied right is imprescriptible and should be regarded as an incident of ownership – part of the bundle of rights which constitutes the ownership of the enclosed piece of ground and so not one that could be lost by non-use.

Civiliter *rule*

A servitude must be exercised in a manner which is least burdensome to the owner of the servient tenement. This has the effect that the owner of the servient tenement's right to enjoy his property should be restricted as little as possible. For example, an owner of a dominant tenement may not widen existing roads or change the route or levels of roads and paths on the servient tenement. Division of the benefited property, such as would occur if a field forming the dominant tenement were to be developed into a number of housing plots for separate ownership, could lead to a proliferation of benefited parties using an servitude access route over the servient tenement and thus a great increase in the burden upon the servient tenement. This would be a clear breach of the *civiliter* rule and the courts would not uphold the increased use.

Extinction of servitudes

Servitudes may be extinguished by:

(1) a *formal written waiver* granted by all the benefited proprietors;

(2) a successful *Lands Tribunal application* by the owner of the servient tenement;

(3) the *non-use* of the servitude for the negative prescriptive period of 20 years (note that this is a different negative prescriptive period from that for real burdens) (but note also the case of *Bowers* v *Kennedy* referred to above for an example of an imprescriptable servitude of necessity);

(4) the *acquiescence* by the owner of the servient servitude with activity by the owner of the dominant servitude inconsistent with the future exercise of the servitude (acquiescence is where consent is given, or no objection is made within a reasonable time, and where the owner of the servient knew or reasonably ought to have known of the activity in question); and

(5) *confusion* of the servient and dominant tenements (which occurs where the benefited and burdened properties come into single ownership – but it is not always clear whether they revive when the ownership is divided again).

LEASES

A lease is a contract whereby heritable property is hired by one party, the tenant, from another, the landlord. At common law, the tenant acquires only a personal right against the landlord, but can acquire a real right if the requirements of the Leases Act 1449 are met. A real right allows the tenant to enforce the lease against the landlord's successors in title. For this to occur, the lease must be in writing; the rent must be specified (a right to occupy heritage without payment is a licence, not a lease); the heritable subjects must be sufficiently identified; there must be an "ish', that is a finite date at which the lease will end and the tenant must have entered into possession of the subjects of the lease. In *Millar* v *McRobbie* (1949) a landowner granted a lease to a farmer over arable land. Prior to the farmer taking up occupancy of the land, the landowner sold it. The purchaser of the land was held not to be bound by the lease, as the tenant had not taken possession, and thus had not acquired a real right.

A real right can also be obtained where the lease is recorded or registered in the property registers (the Register of Sasines or Land Register (see below)).

Rights and duties of landlords

Rights

In addition to the normal contractual remedies of rescission, interdict, implement, damages and eviction, the landlord has additional remedies of irritancy and hypothec (the latter being discussing in Chapter 3). A landlord is entitled to irritate the lease and evict the tenant where the tenant is in arrears of rent for more than 2 years ("legal irritancy") or where specific provision for irritancy is made in the lease ("conventional irritancy"). The tenant has no right to remedy the breach which has led to conventional irritancy (for instance payment of arrears of rent), but the landlord is probably under an obligation not to act oppressively.

Duties

The landlord must give the tenant "full possession" of the subjects. A failure to do so may entitle the tenant to reduce the lease, or at least claim a reduction in the rent. The landlord must also maintain the tenant in possession, that is, he must not derogate from his grant. In *Huber* v *Ross* (1912) a tenant leased a top-floor flat to use as a photographic studio. The landlord carried out structural alterations to the remainder of the tenement which caused considerable damage to the leased flat. The tenant was held entitled not only to repairs to the premises, but also damages for loss of business caused by the works. A landlord must maintain the premises in tenantable condition, and keep the subjects in good repair. In *Gunn* v *NCB* (1982) the tenant was found entitled to damages for loss of clothing and inconvenience and also for loss of wages stemming from asthma brought on by the dampness in the flat he leased from the defenders.

Rights and duties of tenants

Rights

The tenant, like the landlord, is entitled to rescind the lease and to seek interdict or implement to enforce the terms of the lease. The tenant may also be entitled to retain a portion of the rent where the landlord is in breach of his obligations, such as keeping the property in good repair.

Certain other types of lease, notably those relating to residential property are governed by statute rather than common law. These types of leases are beyond the scope of this chapter.

Duties

The tenant must enter into possession of the leased premises and must plenish (furnish) the subjects. The requirement to plenish the subjects is so as to ensure that the landlord has sufficient security for payment of rent should he require to exercise his hypothec (discussed in Chapter 3). The tenant must only use the property for the purposes of the let, he must not "invert the possession". In *Moore* v *Munro* (1896) premises which were leased as a grocer's shop were used by the tenant as a shop on the ground floor and a dwellinghouse on the upper floor. The landlord was held to be barred by acquiescence from preventing the tenant using part of the property as a dwellinghouse, where the valuation roll had referred to the property as "house and shop" for 3 years. The tenant is also obliged to pay rent timeously and to look after the property. In *Fry's Metals* v *Durastic* (1991) tenants who disconnected the alarm system when they left possession of leased subjects were held liable in damages to the landlord when the premises were damaged by vandals.

Essential Facts

- **History of land ownership:** the Scots law of land ownership derives from feudal law and from Roman law which has been laid over the feudal law. This mixture has been much supplemented by statute.

- **Feudal tenure:** in a feudal system of land holding there existed a hierarchy of interests in land with the king at the apex as ultimate superior, with the land occupying vassal at the lowest level, and with one or more mid-superiors. At every level of the hierarchy, the immediate superior is owed a service by the person immediately below them in the hierarchy. Latterly this duty was an annual monetary payment – a "feuduty". A feudal superior could also obtain a payment for agreeing to waive a feudal burden.

- **Abolition of feudal tenure:** between 1970 and 2004, there existed a political movement to abolish feudal tenure. It was considered that feudal superiors with no other interest in a locality were exploiting their vassals economically and stifling the possibility for development. Feudal tenure was finally abolished by the Abolition of Feudal Tenure etc (Scotland) Act 2000. All such tenures came to an end on 28 November 2004.

- **Natural rights in land:** these are rights enshrined in the common law in favour of neighbours and the public and which restrict the freedom that a landowner has to do what he likes with his property.

- **Right of support:** an owner of property has a natural right to expect that the surface of their land will not subside due to the activities of neighbours. Such a right is illustrated (1) by the way the law treats reservations of minerals; and (2) in the law of the tenement.

- **Common law rights ancillary to salmon fishing:** the owner of salmon fishings has rights of access to the fishings over the land of adjoining proprietors. There are also ancillary rights to draw up and moor boats and to wash and hang nets. In each case the owner of the fishings must exercise these rights in the way least injurious to the adjoining proprietor's interests.

- **Water rights:** The channel of streams and rivers is normally owned up to the middle line by the proprietors on either side. The proprietors may use the water for primary domestic purposes but must have regard to the common interest of lower proprietors in the water and sufficient must be left in terms of quality and quantity in the river. The solum of lochs is owned by the adjacent proprietors, who own the land around the shore, up to the middle point. The loch may be used by any of the adjacent proprietors. Where there is an outflow, the proprietors of the loch must have regard for the common interest of proprietors of the lands through which the outflow flows. Water in the sea is not capable of ownership.

- **Regalia:** these are rights held by the Crown in trust for the public. There are two sorts: *regalia majora* are rights which the Crown cannot alienate and exist in the sea, the public interest in the foreshore, and tidal rivers; *regalia minora* are rights which the Crown may alienate and include the right to work and win precious metals of gold, silver and lead, the right to salmon fishings, and certain rights in the foreshore.

- **Nuisance:** this is the right to be able to enjoy an interest in property without having to suffer nuisance or disturbance caused by the proprietors of neighbouring property. Nuisances are disturbances which are out of character for the locality concerned and must be *plus quam tolerabile* before they are actionable.

- **Burdens:** which are imposed contractually (originally feudally) when it is desired to create obligations to be suffered by the proprietor of a burdened property and which benefits the proprietor of a benefited property. They are created in an express deed which must specify the burdened and the benefited properties. The wording of the deed must be clear, unambiguous and sufficient in its terms. Burdens are interpreted narrowly by the courts. Burdens must impose a condition which is of real benefit to enjoyment of the benefited property. They must not give a benefit merely to an individual. Burdens may be distinguished by: minute of waiver, application to the Lands Tribunal; 5-year negative prescription and acquiescence; or by the "sunset rule".

- **Servitudes:** these are title conditions derived from Roman law which are reasonably or absolutely necessary to allow a piece of land to be enjoyed. The benefited land is called the "dominant tenement" while the burdened land is called the "servient tenement". Servitudes must be exercised *civiliter*, that is, in a manner which is least burdensome to the owner of the servient tenement. Servitudes may form overriding interests not disclosed in the Land Register. They are constituted by:

express deed; use followed by positive prescription; or implication and necessity. Servitudes are extinguished by: formal written waiver; application to the Lands Tribunal; non-use or acquiescence followed by negative 20-year prescription; or confusion.

- **Leases:** a lease is a contract whereby heritable property is hired by one party, the tenant, from another, the landlord. At common law, the tenant acquires only a personal right against the landlord, but can acquire a real right if the requirements of the Leases Act 1449 are met. This allows the tenant to enforce the lease against the landlord's successors in title. A real right can also be obtained where the lease is recorded or registered in the property registers (the Register of Sasines or the Land Register).

- **Rights and duties of landlords:** *Rights*: The landlord has the contractual remedies of rescission, interdict, implement, damages and eviction, and the additional remedies of irritancy and hypothec. A landlord may irritate the lease and evict the tenant where the tenant is in arrears of rent for more than 2 years ("legal irritancy") or where specific provision for irritancy is made in the lease ("conventional irritancy"). Conventional irritancy cannot be remedied by the tenant but the landlord should not act oppressively. *Duties*: The landlord must give the tenant "full possession" of the subjects. The landlord must also maintain the tenant in possession. A landlord must maintain the premises in tenantable condition and good repair.

- **Rights and duties of tenants:** *Rights*: The tenant is entitled to rescind the lease, seek interdict or enforce the terms of the lease. The tenant may also be entitled to retain a portion of the rent where the landlord is in breach of his obligations. *Duties*: The tenant must enter into possession of the leased premises and must plenish the subjects. The tenant must only use the property for the purposes of the let, he must not "invert the possession". The tenant must pay rent timeously and look after the property.

Essential Cases

Watt v Jamieson (1954): it was established that to constitute a nuisance a disturbance must be more than can be borne by a reasonable man or woman (*"plus quam tolerabile"*).

Marsden v Craighelen Lawn Tennis and Squash Club (1999): a real burden prohibited the playing of tennis on a Sunday. The court held that a real burden was enforceable only if it was "praedial", that is gave a real benefit to the enjoyment of the benefited property. As a result the court had to decide if the burden was intended to preserve the tranquillity of the Sabbath day (which would be praedial) or whether the original superior simply had strong religious views and did not like frivolous games on the Sabbath (which would not be praedial).

Aberdeen Varieties Ltd v James F Donald (Aberdeen Cinemas) Ltd (1939): the court held that the wording of a burden has to stand on its own and must therefore not refer to something outside the deed which constitutes it. The particular burden referred to in the case was declared invalid since it could only be understand by reference to an Act of Parliament and could not be understood on its own in the absence of the Act.

Bowers v Kennedy (2000): held that a servitude right of access which was absolutely necessary for the access to and thus enjoyment of an enclosed piece of ground was imprescriptable and should be regarded as an incident of ownership and could not be lost by non-use.

Millar v McRobbie (1949): a landowner granted a lease to a farmer over arable land. Prior to the farmer taking up occupancy of the land, the landowner sold it. The purchaser of the land was held not to be bound by the lease, as the tenant had not taken possession, and thus had not acquired a real right.

Huber v Ross (1912): a tenant leased a top-floor flat to use as a photographic studio. The landlord carried out structural alterations to the remainder of the tenement which caused considerable damage to the leased flat. The tenant was held entitled not only to repairs to the premises, but also damages for loss of business caused by the works.

Gunn v NCB (1982): a tenant was found entitled to damages for loss of clothing and inconvenience and also for loss of wages stemming from asthma brought on by the dampness in the flat he leased from the defenders.

Moore v Munro (1896): premises which were leased as a grocer's shop were used by the tenant as a shop on the ground floor and a dwellinghouse on the upper floor. The landlord was barred from preventing the tenant using part of the property as a dwellinghouse, because the valuation roll had referred to the property as "house and shop" for 3 years.

Fry's Metals v Durastic (1991): case tenants who disconnected the alarm system when they left possession of leased subjects were held liable in damages to the landlord when the premises were damaged by vandals.

5 HERITABLE PROPERTY: CONVEYANCING – THE PRACTICAL IMPLICATIONS OF LAND LAW

STAGES IN THE SALE OF HERITABLE PROPERTY

Missives

We saw above that there are usually three stages in the completion of the transfer of heritable property: contract of sale, assignation and delivery. These three stages allow a personal right to develop into a real right. All of these stages are reflected in the sale of interests in land.

When an owner wishes to sell his property, it is first necessary to find a prospective purchaser. This is achieved by marketing the property with an estate agent or solicitor estate agent. From late 2008 onwards, the seller's agents will also require to provide prospective purchasers with a Purchaser's Information Pack (Housing (Scotland) Act 2006) which is intended to ensure that purchasers have information on the condition of the property being sold. It is likely that this will include a seller's survey giving a general value of the property and a view on its condition. In this way the Scottish Parliament has suggested that no separate survey will be required by the purchaser.

Once the property has been viewed by potential purchasers and there appears to be a sufficiency of interest, the sellers will set a closing date for offers. Purchasers will then submit offers which will be collated and considered after the closing date. It is usual for a seller to select the highest offer. An acceptance of the best offer is then prepared. Sometimes, when the property market is sluggish, a property will be offered at a fixed price.

As the original offer will contain a variety of provisions, it is usual for there to be an exchange of qualified acceptances until these provisions have been ironed out. Once there is agreement, the offer and acceptances are completed by the sending of an unqualified acceptance concluding the bargain as between the seller and the purchaser. There then exists *consensus in idem* between the seller and purchaser. The collection of offer and acceptances is known by the collective name of "missives".

The missives will detail the essential terms of the agreement: parties, price, description of the property, and date of entry when the property will change hands. There will be provisions covering what is to happen if the price is not paid in full on the date of entry.

Invariably, there are included in the sale items of moveable property such as carpets, curtains, pelmets, and fitted items such as fitted kitchen units, cookers, dishwashers and other similar appliances. Some of these will be moveable in character and some will be heritable because of accession. For the purposes of Stamp Duty Land Tax (SDLT) payable on a purchase of the heritable items, there may be an apportionment of the price as between heritable and moveable items. This can to some extent be used to reduce the incidence of tax. The missives will state what items are included in the sale and any apportionment.

The purchaser will expect to receive a good and marketable title and there will be provisions to this effect in the missives. Apart from warranties as to title, the purchaser will also wish to see that statutory restrictions have been complied with. It is usual for a seller to obtain property enquiry certificates from the local authority confirming the planning, building control, water, drainage and roads position. In this way the purchaser is able to see that the property is in an area designated for planning purposes with an appropriate zoning, allowing the intended use, and that there are no adverse planning decisions or intentions on the local and structure plans. Building control will indicate if there are any statutory notices issued (such as for repairs), that the building complies with the Building Acts provisions, confirming that any alterations or additions to the property have received a building warrant and completion certificate. The roads department will confirm whether or not the road and footpath skirting the property have been taken over for maintenance by the local authority. The water and drainage department can confirm whether the property is served with a public water supply or a private supply of a wholesome standard, and also that the property benefits from a public sewer or a septic tank for the disposal of waste. Missives will also deal with any remedial works carried out to the property for the eradication of damp, rot or infestations and ensure that the benefit of any guarantee is transferred to the purchaser.

The missives will also provide how the provisions of the Matrimonial Homes (Family Protection) (Scotland) Act 1981 (as amended) are to be fulfilled. The Act gives rights of occupancy to any spouse or civil partner who resides in the property along with the seller but where the spouse or civil partner concerned is not noted in the title certificate or documents as a co-owner. The seller must issue formal documentation that there is no spouse or civil partner with occupancy rights, that the property is not a matrimonial home within the meaning of the Act, or the seller must provide consents by any such spouse or civil partner to the sale or alternatively a renunciation by the spouse or civil partner of any occupancy rights.

The missives will confirm that there are no restrictions on the seller's power to transfer ownership, on what searches are to be conducted and the form of any documents to be delivered including the disposition in favour of the purchaser. The missives should also detail what is to happen in the event of breach of contract by either party and especially where there is any delay in settlement.

Missives are therefore complex and technical and we have given merely an overview of their typical terms. However, the great advantage of missives is that they comprise a binding contract between the seller and the purchaser and therefore can be used as a basis for court action in the event of a material breach of contract and on their strength either party can enforce the other party to fulfil their obligations or alternatively sue for damages in the event that the other party cannot or will not fulfil their obligations. The case of *Rodger (Builders) Ltd* v *Fawdry* (1950) illustrates how an ultimatum procedure is standardly used in the courts to demand performance of a material obligation which has been breached.

Following the conclusion of missives, the seller will send to the purchaser the title certificate and any other relevant title documentation relating to the property, together also with evidences of the warranties made in the missives. The seller will proceed to arrange for the discharge of any existing standard security over the property and the purchaser will arrange for finance of the purchase and the preparation of their own standard security. Other settlement documents may also require to be prepared including the documents instructing searches to ensure that the seller is not prevented from completing the sale and that the title is not encumbered with any diligences or charges which would prevent the sale from being completed. For a more detailed treatment, see John Sinclair, *Conveyancing Practice in Scotland* (4th edn, 2002).

The disposition and its clauses

The second stage in transferring ownership to the property is effected by the drafting by the purchaser's solicitor and execution by the seller of the disposition. This is the formal document which transfers ownership of the heritable property into the name of the seller. So far as the title to the heritable property is concerned, the disposition supersedes the provisions in the missives. Dispositions generally are of a standard form and typically include the following standard clauses:

(1) The *narrative clause*: which narrates formally the names of the seller and purchaser and the amount of the sale price.

(2) The *dispositive clause*: this clause divests the seller of their title and invests the purchaser of the title. As a result it contains a formal description of the property. (We examine descriptions in more detail below.) It is normal for the dispositive clause to end with the following three clauses: "together with (First) the whole rights, parts, privileges and pertinents relating to the said subjects; (Two) the whole fixtures and fittings therein and thereon; and (Three) my whole right, title and interest, present and future, therein and thereto". The functions of these "catch-all" clauses are to ensure respectively that (1) the purchaser acquires all the rights to all the parts of the property sold and also the rights over neighbouring properties as are necessary to enjoy the property to the full; (2) the sale includes the building and fixtures and moveables which have been built or acceded to the property and also that any moveable fittings are included; and (3) the whole rights of the seller are transferred to the purchaser including any rights which may arise in the future – that is, that it is a full and unreserved divesting of the seller and investing of the purchaser.

(3) the *burdens clause*: in which any burdens or express servitudes are stated either by repetition in full or by reference to the documents which created them – such inclusion does not certify that the burdens are still valid or applicable – for those issues, the purchaser's solicitor must use his judgement;

(4) the *entry clause*: which warrants entry to the property at the specified time (usually the date on which the price is payable). It is usual for this clause to state that entry is given with vacant possession and actual occupation – in other words, that no part of the property is subject to lets or occupation by any other party.

(5) the *warrandice clause*: this clause is a guarantee to the seller by the purchaser and also operates to assign to the purchaser the guarantees which were in their turn made to the seller. There are three forms of warrandice: (1) absolute warrandice ("And I grant warrandice") which is an unrestricted guarantee of title; (2) Fact and deed warrandice which is a guarantee given (usually by a person in an administrative capacity such as a trustee or executor) that they have not and will not do any act prejudicial to the purchaser's interests and usually they bind the estate under their charge in absolute warrandice ("And I grant warrandice from my own facts and deeds

only and bind the executry estate under my charge in absolute warrandice"); and (3) simple warrandice which is a guarantee that the granter of the disposition has not done anything to the prejudice of the grantee (this is the usual clause where a gift of the property is given – the granter is saying to the grantee that he takes the property with all its faults and holds it just as he did) ("And I grant simple warrandice"). The importance of warrandice is that in the event that there is a defect in the title, the purchaser can sue the previous owners under the guarantee and recover damages.

(6) the *certificate of value*: this clause was included for the purposes of assessing the band and rate of stamp duty which was applicable to the disposition. However, stamp duty land tax is no longer administered in a way which requires such a clause.

(7) the *testing clause*: the purchaser will complete this clause which narrates the place and date of signing of the disposition and the name and designation of the witness or witnesses. The Requirements of Writing (Scotland) Act 1995, s 3(1) states that a disposition by an individual will be valid if it is signed by that individual on the last page (and the last page of any schedule or plan annexed) and that the same is witnessed by one witness to the signing.

In addition to these standard clauses, there are certain other implied clauses. For example there is an assignation of rents, whereby a seller transfers to the purchaser all right competent to them to demand rents from any tenants from on and after the date of entry.

Registration and recording

Delivery of the disposition on the date of settlement completes the divesting of the seller and the vesting of the purchaser. It is therefore vitally important that the whole clauses in the missives have been fulfilled but there are usually certain matters which are still outstanding. For this reason, the seller's solicitor usually grants a letter of obligation binding the seller to deliver any outstanding documentation to the purchaser's solicitor. This usually involves formal obligations necessary to ensure that the purchaser will be able to register the disposition and title in his own name and receive a land certificate showing him to be the proprietor and that the property is (or at least will be) clear of any charges such as the seller's standard security which is being discharged.

The purchaser thereafter completes an application to the Land Register and forwards to the Keeper the application Form 1, the disposition and any other documents such as the purchaser's standard security so that the Keeper will register the purchaser as proprietor and the purchaser's creditor as holder of a charge over the property.

It is this registration of the title which completes the third stage of the transfer of the heritable property into the name of the purchaser and which finally converts the personal rights into real rights. Some words about registration need to be included at this stage.

Registration and recording of title/title deeds

The current system of completion of title requires registration of all dispositions where there is a transfer for value of an interest in land. This is provided for by the Land Registration (Scotland) Act 1979 (s 2(1)(a)(ii): there are also certain other situations which require registration). While registration of title was introduced in 1979, it was not possible to operate a Scotland-wide transfer of property into the new Land Register. Instead registration was introduced on a county-by-county basis over the following 20 or so years.

The need for a state involvement in completion of title to land was first recognised in the Registration Act 1617. This Act was passed to prevent owners of property from selling it to others, receiving large sums of money for the property, but thereafter fraudulently dispossessing the purchasers and recovering the land in question. The exact details of the frauds need not concern us, but we can appreciate the difficulties of relying on a succession of deeds to land for providing us with assurance of ownership in the absence of a formal system of registration. To prevent such fraud, the 1617 Act provides for the creation of a public register of deeds to land. Such a register could be searched to establish what deeds affect which interest land, and thus we could identify the deeds relating to any particular piece of land in the country. This process was greatly enhanced by the creation of comprehensive indices of land and also (later) of persons. Such a system of recording of deeds continued until replaced by the Land Register after 1979. The register was known as the General Register of Sasines which was divided into 33 counties across Scotland.

The General Register of Sasines

The General Register of Sasines was a register of deeds and, as such, it merely noted the terms of the recorded deeds but did not guarantee their authenticity or validity. As a result, it was quite possible for a deed to be struck at in a court action for reduction of the deed and thus shown to have no legal effect. For example, a proprietor of land might be induced by fraud to sign over their property to a grantee. By raising an action seeking reduction of the fraudulent disposition, and on the court receiving sufficient proof of the fraud, the court would grant decree of reduction of the disposition which would thus be shown to have no validity. However, the disposition will have been recorded in the Register of Sasines. The original granter would be able to record the court decree in the same register against the interest in land and this would publicise the reduction of the deed and would act to show that the original granter was not lawfully divested of the property but is still entitled to be regarded as the lawful proprietor with all the rights that flowed from that ownership.

It follows from this that in order to be satisfied that any particular title was valid, it was necessary for a purchaser to examine the progress of titles shown on the relative search sheet in the Register of Sasines (indices of transmissions with the relative interest in land) and thus, by looking back far enough, the purchaser would know that no other party had a competing claim to the interest in land concerned. A difficulty was the question of how far back was it necessary to search? The answer to this question was provided by the law of prescription. The Prescription and Limitation (Scotland) Act 1973, s 1 provides that the relative period concerned was a full period of 10 years and that therefore "If land has been possessed by any person, or by any person and his successors, for a continuous period of ten years openly, peaceably and without judicial interruption" and was founded upon a deed which appears valid and sufficient in its terms to include the interest in land concerned, then the right in question will be exempt from challenge. This led to the practice of checking the title deeds shown on the search sheets back for period of at least 10 years (in fact back to the first deed outwith the 10-year period) for completeness and validity. In this way it could be ascertained that there was no party who could raise a competent challenge based on a competing deed (for if a person made a claim based upon an earlier deed, no court would entertain any such claim). The practice also emphasises the importance of examining the search against the interest in the land concerned. In practice while the principal search sheet was kept in the General Register of Sasines at Meadowbank House in Edinburgh, copies of this could be obtained from the Keeper or from a firm of insured professional searchers. The title of any property would therefore include a progress of titles of over 10 years in duration and also a "search for incumbrances" relating to the interest in land. At the time of a sale, the search would need to be brought up to date to show that there were no recent deeds or diligences prejudicial to the new proprietor's interests. This was achieved by instructing a continuation of the search and of an interim report on the search which would be examined as close to the date of entry as possible. The letter of obligation would include an obligation to deliver in due course a search for incumbrances brought forward in the property and personal registers to show no deed or diligence prejudicial to the interests of the purchaser. The reference to personal registers refers to the fact that it is possible for a creditor to obtain an Inhibition and certain other court diligences which prevent a person from selling their property, giving their property in security, or otherwise dealing with their property until the diligence is recalled. Such diligences would not appear on the property register but would appear on a separate register of persons. The prescriptive period for diligences was shorter, at 5 years. It was therefore necessary for searches in the personal register to be made against all persons having any interest in the land within the 10-year (property) period to be searched against for a period of 5 years prior to disposing of the property. In this way the purchaser could be assured that there was nothing to prevent that person from disposing of the property at the time of that disposal. It is now possible to see why it is necessary in missives to include references to searches in the property and personal registers being continued and being clear.

While the Register of Sasines was a register of deeds (any one of which, in the right circumstances, could be reduced and shown to have no validity), the intention with Land Registration was to do away with the need to check a progress of deeds and searches by replacing the Register of Sasines with the new Land Register.

The Land Register

The Land Register is not a register of deeds. It is a register of state guaranteed titles. The Keeper on receiving an application for the registration of a title will carry out a checking exercise to confirm the validity of the progress of deeds and will also check searches. As a result the Keeper can issue a land certificate which guarantees that the proprietor in possession of the interest in land is the owner with all the rights that go with that ownership. The land certificate comprises a number of separate sections:

(1) the *property* section: this shows an ordnance survey plan of the appropriate scale with the interest in land outlined in red and which section also provides a brief description using the postal address and possibly reference to a deed containing a full conveyancing description;

(2) the *proprietorship* section: this details the proprietors having an interest in the land;

(3) the *charges* section: this details the interest of any heritable creditor holding a standard security; and

(4) the *burdens* section: this details the burdens relating to the land by means first of identifying the recorded deed which created the burden and then the terms of the burden copied word for word from that deed. It should be noted that not all title conditions will appear in the burdens section. A servitude arising by implication, prescription or necessity will not have been created by an express deed and will therefore not appear on the land certificate. It is one of a number of recognised "overriding interests" which are not noted.

In the event of any ambiguity arising, the Keeper can exclude indemnity of the title to the extent of that ambiguity. It will be seen that prescription still has a role to play in that where there is exclusion of indemnity, such exclusion will persist only for the prescriptive 10-year period after which, if there has been no challenge made, the Keeper can rectify the land certificate to remove the exclusion of indemnity.

A registered title with no exclusion of indemnity held by a proprietor in possession is therefore to all intents and purposes said to be invulnerable. It matters not whether the deed which triggered registration is subsequently reduced. Such reduction will have no effect on the validity of the registered title. This is illustrated in the case of *Kaur* v *Singh* (1999). The pursuer claimed that the disposition in favour of the defender was invalid in that her signature had been forged. She sought reduction of the disposition. There was a struggle by the pursuer to gain possession of the property which finally failed. As the defender had a registered title and had possession he could not be dispossessed of the property. Even if reduction of the disposition had been possible, it would have had no effect on the registered title. However, in *Short's Tr* v *Chung (No 2)* (1998), a trustee in sequestration claimed that the defender's property was part of the bankrupt estate and that the defender had acquired title by means of a gratuitous alienation made by the sequestrated party. The trustee sought a court order ordaining the defender to execute a disposition in favour of the trustee and thus gained possession of the property.

Coupled with the idea of a guaranteed title, is that where a party is subsequently shown to have a valid claim in relation to the registered title and to have suffered loss as a result, such a person can claim compensation from the Keeper. Of course, it is necessary for such a person to establish that they have suffered loss and possibly also to quantify the loss they have suffered.

Apart from removing an exclusion of indemnity, the Keeper's powers to rectify a registered title is very limited. Rectification by the Keeper is provided for in s 9 of the 1979 Act and is restricted to four situations:

(1) to note an overriding interest or correct an entry relating to an overriding interest;

(2) where all persons likely to be affected by the change have been notified and consented to the rectification;

(3) where the inaccuracy has been caused by the fraud or carelessness of the proprietor in possession; or

(4) where the rectification relates to a matter where indemnity has been excluded.

There are other situations where rectification of the register may appear appropriate. One of these occurs where there is a dispute between neighbouring proprietors about the boundaries shown on their respective titles. In theory this should not happen, but for reasons we look at in the next section, this can occur and s 19 of the 1979 Act provides that where the titles to adjoining lands disclose a discrepancy as to the common boundary, the proprietors concerned can reach an agreement acceptable to them both and register the agreed plan with a docket or agreement attached in the Land Register (and Register of Sasines where appropriate) and the Keeper will note the terms of that agreement accordingly which will thereafter be binding on both proprietors and their successors in their respective interests.

DESCRIPTIONS

To be effective, the disposition of any interest in land must contain an adequate description of the interest conveyed. What is meant by an "adequate description" has varied over the years.

Descriptions in the Sasine Register

Immediately prior to the introduction of registration of title, the standard expected was a high one, but conveyancers frequently fell somewhat short of this standard.

Broadly speaking, a description is either a particular description or a general description. A particular description is one which specifies the boundaries of the property owned and limits the possession of the owner to those boundaries. It is not possible for the owner of the land to acquire right to any land beyond the specified boundary by means of occupation and prescription as the title is specific and does not allow of that. A general description, on the other hand is not specific and therefore depends upon actual possession of the land and prescription to fortify the ownership.

Particular descriptions

Practice has created several ways of achieving a particular description. Usually this is achieved by giving a precise *verbal description* of the property sufficient to identify all the boundaries with precision by reference to fixed points and features on the land. Usually this is achieved using a *bounding description*. By convention, boundaries are usually narrated clockwise from the most northerly point. Here is an example of a bounding description:

> "All and whole that plot or area of ground in Vine Place, Edinburgh in the County of Midlothian, extending to 0.75 acres or thereby Imperial Measure and bounded as follows: On or towards the North by the road known as Vine Place, Edinburgh along which it extends One hundred and sixty feet or thereby Imperial measure; thereafter on or towards the East by the centre line of the existing mutual wall separating the property hereby disponed from the property known as number 19 Vine Place Edinburgh along which it extends Two hundred feet or thereby Imperial measure; thereafter on the South by the centre line of the existing mutual wall separating the property hereby disponed from the back gardens of the properties known as numbers 6 and 8 Vine Quadrant, Edinburgh along which it extends One hundred and sixty feet or thereby Imperial measure; and finally on or towards the West by the existing stob and wire fence and partly by the hedge separating the property hereby disponed from the property known as number 15 Vine Place, Edinburgh along which it extends Two hundred feet or thereby Imperial measure."

It will be seen that this description for a specified rectangular piece of ground of a defined area is specified by reference to the ground features which comprise the measured boundary features. Anyone visiting the site would be able to identify the precise boundaries. There is no room for doubt. One problem which crops up from time to time is the question of whether the boundary features are included in the property or excluded. The general rule is that if a property is defined as "bounded by" a feature then that feature is excluded from the property. The property goes up to that feature but does not include it. However, where a boundary is said to be mutual then the actual boundary is the middle line (*"medium filum"*) of that feature. In the above example, the road and pavement are excluded from the property, while the walls, fence and hedge are included up to their middle line. A fuller treatment of this is summarised in Burns, *Conveyancing Practice* (1957). In a proper particular description, there is therefore no room for ambiguity and the title is not capable of allowing the owner to acquire any interest in land beyond the boundary by means of prescription.

A particular description very often will be achieved by using plans together with a bounding description or as a substitute for a bounding description. Plans may be *taxative* or *demonstrative only*. To be specific, a taxative plan should show the cardinal points of the compass, the orientation of the plot on the ground within the context of neighbouring land features, the boundaries of the plot clearly outlined with measured sides, and include any fixed ground features. All too often, an otherwise perfect taxative plan includes no fixed points or other fixed boundary features and is therefore merely a "floating rectangle" incapable of adequately specifying a description of the land in question. This is a typical conveyancer's error and features in a number of prominent court cases. To complete the description in the disposition, it is necessary to refer to the plot as shown on the plan, for example: "outlined in red and coloured pink on the taxative plan annexed and executed as relative hereto." Care should be taken to avoid any contradiction between the plan and the verbal terms in the description clause. But if there is any such contradiction or ambiguity, a taxative plan will overrule the verbal description. Where a plan is defined as "demonstrative only and not taxative" then it will perform a useful function in illustrating in graphic form the plot and its boundaries, but the plan will not overrule the verbal description contained in the disposition. In all cases the plans should be drawn to an identifiable scale. At one time it was considered that a plan drawn up by a surveyor was the best form of description available, but there are well-known problems with any plan-based system to which we shall return below within this section.

Once a description has been particularly defined, it is perfectly good practice to describe the interest in land conveyed in a disposition by making reference to the deed in which the interest is particularly defined. For example:

> "ALL and WHOLE that dwellinghouse and garden ground known as and forming number 17 Vine Place, Edinburgh in the County of Midlothian being the subjects particularly described in and disponed by and delineated and coloured pink on the plan annexed and executed as relative to the disposition by Edward Jenkins and Mrs. Eleanor Gosforth or Jenkins in my favour dated 23rd November and recorded in the

Division of the General Register of Sasines applicable to the County of Midlothian on 5th December all in the year Nineteen hundred and eighty four" (Conveyancing (Scotland) Act 1924, s 8).

General descriptions

A general description is one which names or describes property generally but fails to be specific in defining the boundaries or any of them. At one time, properties were identified locally by a general name, for example "Gladstone's Land" is a 17th-century tenement owned by the National Trust for Scotland and situated in the Lawnmarket, Edinburgh. The tenement is well known locally by that name and if one visited the tenement its boundaries would be easily ascertainable. Similar general names are frequently encountered in country properties, for example: "All and Whole the Barony of ..." or "All and Whole the farm and lands of ...". In all of these cases, which were no doubt perfectly adequate in former times, it can be difficult to state what are the precise boundaries of the property possessed. Where there is such doubt, it is necessary to ascertain the areas, fields and buildings actually occupied by the owner and any tenants. Where there is ambiguity a piece of ground which is capable of being included under the general description may be acquired by means of prescription. That is to say, by means of occupation for the full 10-year prescriptive period, openly, peaceably and without judicial interruption. But a general description is clearly inferior to a particular description and is to be avoided where possible.

Other forms of general description include: (1) a description by means only of a postal address; (2) a description which would be particular but for some ambiguity in expression along one or more of its boundaries; and (3) the description of a flat.

Flats give rise to particular problems. They defy the general principle that an owner possesses the land *a coelo usque ad centrum* (from the heavens above to the centre of the earth). However, a general description stating the orientation of the flat within the tenement is regarded as sufficient. For example:

"All and Whole that southmost second floor dwellinghouse entering by the common passage and stair number 13 Wardlaw Street, Edinburgh in the County of Midlothian."

Such are the forms of description contained in dispositions in the Sasine Register and which will be encountered in a disposition giving rise to a first registration in the Land Register. The situation in the Land Register itself is different.

Descriptions in the Land Register

When a property is subject to registration in the Land Register, the
Keeper will attempt to transfer the existing conveyancing descriptions
to an appropriately scaled Ordnance Survey plan. Three scales are used
1:10,000, 1:2500 and 1:1250. The largest scale is generally used for
urban properties. Even so, the plans often do not admit of very clear
specification of the boundary features and in the absence of a verbal
description details of the measurements of boundaries, the nature of
the bounding feature and the issue of whether the bounding feature
is outside the land or mutual may not be specified. The information
required to be shown on the title certificate plan is detailed in the
Registration of Title Book published electronically on the Registers of
Scotland website (http://www.ros.gov.uk/rotbook). Paragraph 4.4 of
the *Registration of Title Book* describes the minimum contents as follows:
"The title and certificate plan will delineate the property and may also,
by use of different colouring or hatching, indicate parts feued or parts
let on long lease, parts affected by certain burdens, rights of access or
parts of the registered interest which have been conveyed away." A
brief verbal description is also used but this is usually little more than
a postal address. Clearly, the transfer of legal descriptions is a matter of
judgement. To assist in this judgement, the Keeper will compare the
legal title expressed in previous deeds and where relevant shown on
plans annexed to such deeds with the Ordnance Survey plan. He will
also compare the interest being registered with the registered titles to
surrounding land. At this stage discrepancies are frequently encountered
between the interest occupied on the ground and the interest described
in the legal documentation. Sometimes there is insufficient information
given to identify the ground features needed to tie the legal description
to the Ordnance Survey plan. Some of these discrepancies may
appear small enough for them to be effectively ignored – covered by
the "or thereby" principle. Other discrepancies may require a formal
comparison between the occupational boundaries and the Ordnance
Survey plan. On a first registration it is usual to obtain a P16 report so
that the physical boundaries can be checked against the ordnance survey
plan for the area. Once the judgment exercise has been carried out,
the title certificate should show the property on the Ordnance Survey
plan, delineating the boundaries, and the verbal description should
ideally indicate the rights in those boundaries and any additional rights
common, mutual or otherwise which are included in the ownership of
the land.

As a result of the description in the title certificate, dispositions of land defined in the Land Register need be no more than a simple postal description combined with a reference to the Title Sheet number, for example: "ALL and WHOLE the piece of ground with the dwellinghouse erected thereon known as number Fifteen Nile Street, Glasgow in the County of Renfrew and being the subjects registered under title number REN98765." The Keeper does not check the titles of the adjacent sasine properties and so it is quite possible for errors and inaccuracies to occur and for these to go completely unnoticed. However, in the event of agreement between neighbours as to the line of the actual boundary, a plan may be agreed under s 19 of the Land Registration (Scotland) Act 1979. Such plan with its accompanying docket or agreement can be registered in the Land Register or recorded in the Register of Sasines and is definitive of the agreement which has been reached.

Problems with map-based descriptions

When the Land Registration (Scotland) Act 1979 was enacted, those who envisaged the system considered that description of land by reference to a scale plan was the most objective method of defining boundary features. This is, however, not so.

It is well known that plans and maps suffer from irresolvable inaccuracies which do in fact impinge upon the accuracy of land descriptions. For example:

(1) *Projection distortion*: since the earth is round and not flat, lines of latitude and longitude are not straight. When geographical information is transferred to a two dimensional plan there is always some level of expansion as one moves to the edges of a plan. Distances at the edges of a plan are stretched. To some extent this error can be minimised by using maps at the largest possible scale.

(2) *Photographic distortion*: since maps are prepared from aerial photographs, there are always some areas of distortion due to the effect of refraction in camera lenses. Features at the edges of the photograph will be being photographed at an oblique angle rather than directly from above. Other forms of photographic distortion include film and print shrinkage, and even the effect of atmospheric distortion. All of these photographic effects give rise to distortion of plans made from aerial photographs.

(3) *Photographic interpretation*: some ground features such as fences are in fact invisible on aerial photographs due to their small area of incidence. Such features are drawn on plans as interpretations of

the cartographer implied by the change in texture between fields and plots of ground rather than as visible features. This adds to the inaccuracy of plotted boundary features.

(4) *Gradient*: the earth's surface is not flat while that image on a plan is. A square field on the side of a hill with all sides of equal measurement will look shorter on the sides with the rising gradient when seen from above – and when shown on a plan (which is prepared from aerial photography). This is the same effect as that which causes a penny to look elliptical rather than round when viewed at an angle.

(5) *Plotting exaggerations*: in transferring information from photographs to plans, certain features, rivers, roads, paths, walls and fences, and even buildings are drawn onto plans at much greater than actual size. If they were drawn at actual size, many of these ground features would not be visible on the plans. An example of this occurs when the width of boundary walls shown on Ordnance Survey plans is calculated. On a 1:1250 plan a line drawn 1 millimetre thick corresponds to a ground feature 1.25 metres in width. The thinnest lines used on 1:1250 plans are generally recognised to have a thickness of 25 cm on the ground (around 10 inches).

(6) *Cumulative errors*: the sum total of the above errors and distortions may mean that any particular point shown on a 1:250 plan may have a cumulative inaccuracy of around 5 metres when compared with its actual position on the ground.

Some of these errors cause "absolute inaccuracy" (affecting the true position of the feature on the earth's surface) but for the purposes of land disputes what is more important is "relative accuracy" (the position of ground features on a map shown in relation to neighbouring ground features on the map should closely reflect the position of actual ground features on the surface in relation to neighbouring ground features on the surface). In connection with boundary disputes, a certain amount of inaccuracy can be tolerated, but the larger the areas of land owned, the greater the inaccuracy. This means that the boundaries of country estates may be difficult to specify from Ordnance Survey plans at 1:10,000 scale and this can have a crucial effect in the resolution of a dispute.

It follows that the standard of accuracy used by the Land Register may already be insufficient to resolve some disputes. Apart from the costs of administration and the availability of resources there is no reason why the current map based system could not be enhanced by the adoption of a digital cadastral mapping system based upon GPS triangulation. It is generally held that a point identified by cadastral mapping has a

5-centimetre accuracy. It is likely that future versions of the Ordnance Survey plans will be prepared using digital cadastral mapping to reduce the photographic distortions referred to above. Other distortions are likely to remain a feature of any map based land registration system.

LAW OF THE TENEMENT

In a tenement of separate flats where different storeys belong to different people, there is a need to identify the responsibility of owners for common facilities such as passageways, stairs, back greens and garden ground, roofs, foundations, gables and external walls.

In tenement titles after the mid-19th century, these items are likely to be referred to in the title deeds of the flats along with some formula as to how the costs of maintenance, repair and renewal are to be apportioned and shared out among the proprietors of each flat in the tenement. Very often the sharing of such costs will be in the proportion to which the feuduty of the individual flats relates to the cumulo feuduty of the tenement as a whole. Sometimes, rateable value is used instead of feuduty.

However, such apportionment regimes set out to avoid the inequitable situations in earlier times created by the common law provisions known as the "law of the tenement" which allocated responsibility for common items to the proprietors who had ownership and thus control over those items adjacent to their flats. For the law of the tenement, see Rankine, *Land Ownership* (4th edn, 1909), pp 661ff.

For example, under the law of the tenement:

(1) the proprietor of the ground-floor flat owns the ground ("*solum*") and foundations upon which the tenement is built and so the proprietor of the ground-floor flat owes a duty of support to the proprietors of the upper flats. The proprietor of the ground-floor flat therefore bears the responsibility for maintenance of the solum and foundations and must bear the costs of doing so;

(2) the proprietors of the flats in the tenement own the external walls enclosing their flats and which walls provide support for the upper storeys. As owners of those enclosing walls they are likewise under a duty to maintain their walls and thus must bear the costs of doing so;

(3) the proprietor of the top flat has the ownership of the roof space and roof and thus owes a duty to the other proprietors of keeping the roof wind and water tight and structurally in good order. It follows

that the responsibility for maintenance of the roof falls on the top flat proprietor who must bear the costs of the upkeep of the roof;

(4) the responsibility for gables, walls and ceilings likewise falls to be divided by the proprietors of the flats between which such features physically exist;

(5) the responsibility for the common passage and stairs is born by those proprietors whose properties are served by them;

(6) the proprietor of the ground-floor flat not only owns the solum but, in accordance with the principle of ownership *a coelo usque ad centrum* (from the heavens above to the centre of the earth), also owns the air space above the roof of the tenement. As a result, the owner of the top flat is not allowed to extend the tenement upwards; and

(7) in the event that the tenement is totally destroyed by fire, the proprietor of the ground-floor flat, as owner of the solum, has the right to say what is to be done with the land. He may decide to rebuild the tenement or not. The proprietors of the other flats have no say in the matter.

This ownership- and duty-based system, while very logical in conception, placed a very considerable burden on certain proprietors and took no account of the fact that all of the proprietors in the tenement obtained the benefit of the maintenance of such common items and so perhaps should bear an equitable share of the costs. Arguably, the proprietor of the top flat was the most prejudiced in that roof repairs can involve very considerable costs.

While one would expect an equitable apportionment of costs in title deeds granted after the mid-19th century, this did not resolve the fact that with older tenements the law of the tenement still applied. It was always one of the responsibilities of a conveyancer to check that the costs of repairs to common items were shared on some equitable basis and missives usually had a clause stipulating that this was to be the case. In the unlucky event that an older tenement was involved, a purchaser would have to think long and hard and check the condition of the roof and structure before committing himself to purchase a flat where the law of the tenement applied in default of any equitable title provisions.

However, the situation has recently been amended by the Tenements (Scotland) Act 2004 which enacts a new regime applying by default wherever the title deeds of a tenement are silent as to the apportionment of responsibility and costs of maintenance of common items. Where the provision in title deeds is silent in relation to some of the common items, the product may be that some common items are dealt with as provided for in the title deeds and other common items are provided for under the new statutory regime. Under the new statutory regime, while the ownership of the solum, walls, gables, roofs, and so on remain with the adjacent proprietor (so that the owner of the top flat owns the roof space above the flat), the responsibility for maintenance falls to be carried out by the whole proprietors. Rule 1.2 to the First Schedule to the 2004 Act states that any property common to two or more proprietors, the ground on which the tenement is built, the foundations, the external walls, roof, gables and any load bearing walls are designated as "scheme property" and the costs of such scheme property will be shared equally among the whole proprietors. In cases where flats are of different sizes the costs may be shared on the basis of floor area. Thus the new statutory regime acknowledged the ownership element of the law of the tenement but transfers the duty element to the whole proprietors of the tenement.

Essential Facts

- **Missives:** these consist of an exchange of formal letters comprising an original offer and one or more acceptances taken together. Missives therefore form an enforceable contract for the sale of land and buildings, together with the moveable items included in the sale. The rights and obligations which arise under missives are personal rights and obligations. More is needed to convert personal rights in the land and buildings into real rights. Missives will detail the essential terms of the agreement: parties, price, description of the property, and date of entry when the property will change hands. They also include a very wide range of other technical provisions. Common clauses include: the apportionment of price as between heritable property and moveable property; clauses imposing interest and other consequences in the event of delayed payment of the price; clauses relating to the fulfilment of matrimonial homes documentation; clauses confirming the status of the property for the purposes of planning status, statutory building notices, environmental matters including water and sewerage services, roads, utilities, good and marketable title, and many other matters.
- **Dispositions:** the formal conveyance of the heritable property (which when delivered supersedes the conditions in the missives concerning heritable property) is known as a disposition and includes

a number of standard clauses: narrative, dispositive, burdens (in a conveyance of a registered title there is no need to refer to burdens since these are specified in the Land Register), entry clause, warrandice clause and testing clause.

- **The Land Register:** the Land Register is a register of state guaranteed titles to land. Where a property has hitherto not been registered in the Land Register, an application for a first registration is required to complete the title. The purchasing solicitor will check the progress of title deeds over the full prescriptive ten year period and will also examine the existing search in the property register. The application for first registration will be accompanied by the title deeds and the Keeper will carry out a similar check on the title deeds. The description in the title deeds will need to be compared with the ordnance survey map at the appropriate scale.

- **The Land Certificate:** when the Keeper is satisfied that the title deeds on a first registration constitute a good title, he will issue a Land Certificate to the proprietor. The land certificate is in four parts: the property section which defines the interest in land owned using a plan at the appropriate scale; the proprietorship section identifying the proprietor; the charges section identifying the heritable creditors; and the burdens section identifying the deeds which impose burdens and repeating the terms of burdens verbatim. In the event of any ambiguity, the Keeper can exclude indemnity of the title to the extent of the ambiguity. The Keeper can rectify the registered title in four limited circumstances: (1) to note an overriding interest; (2) where all parties affected consent; (3) where there has been fraud or carelessness by the proprietor; and (4) where the rectification relates to a matter where indemnity has been excluded. In a dispute over the registered title, the proprietor in possession of the property is in a privileged position. In the event of a claim that some party has suffered loss, the courts cannot reduce the registered title, but the Keeper can indemnify that party by paying them compensation.

- **The Register of Sasines:** this is the older register of deeds. In the event that a disposition in favour of the owner is invalid, the disposition can be reduced by the court in an action of reduction. If the pursuer is successful, this his has the effect is causing the owner to lose his title to the property.

- **Descriptions in the Land Register:** the definition of the property interest owned is achieved by reference to an ordnance survey plan at the appropriate scale. Plan-based systems such as this suffer from a degree of inaccuracy as a result of a number of geometrical and physical distortions and exaggerations.

- **Descriptions in the Sasine Register:** descriptions are generally verbal but may be assisted by plans. Descriptions are divided into two types: particular or general. Particular descriptions are specific and may be achieved by a bounding description verbally identifying all the boundaries by reference to ground features and often including measurements. Such descriptions are often supplemented by plans which may be taxative or demonstrative. Where there is a contradiction between the plan and the deed, a taxative plan will have priority while a demonstrative plan will not. General descriptions are little more than indications of the property and may be achieved by: (1) a general name; (2) a postal address; or (3) the description of the storey and orientation of a flat within a tenement. General descriptions need not be ineffective and often the exact boundaries can be identified by examination of the walls and other boundary features on the ground at the site.

- **Law of the tenement:** the old common law provides that the owner of the *solum*, the owner of the ground flat, is under a duty to provide the owners of the flats above with support and so must maintain the walls enclosing the flat and the foundations at his expense. Similarly, owners of other flats have to maintain their enclosing walls which provide support to the flats above them. The owner of the top flat owns the roof and roof space but is under a duty to maintain the roof for the benefit of all the lower flats. The burden of the costs of maintaining the roof has long been regarded as inequitable. As a result, since the mid-19th century, it is common for title deeds of tenement flats to stipulate that the costs of maintenance of all common items will be shared on some equitable basis. Recently, the law of the tenement has been amended statutorily by the Tenements (Scotland) Act 2004. Under the new statutory regime, while the ownership of the solum, walls, gables, roofs, and so on remain with the adjacent proprietor (so that the owner of the top flat owns the roof space above the flat), the responsibility for maintenance falls to be carried out by the whole proprietors. The statutory regime comes into play only when the title deeds are silent about maintenance of the common items.

Essential Cases

Rodger (Builders) Ltd v Fawdry (1950): the court approved an ultimatum procedure to be applied where there is a material breach of missives. A defaulting party is given a reasonable time the obligation, the date for performance of which has passed. After the expiry of this reasonable time, an ultimatum will be given requiring performance within a further reasonable time period. If performance has still not taken place by the end of this second reasonable time period, then the pursuer may rescind from the contract, regard the contract as being at an end and sue for damages.

Kaur v Singh (1999): the pursuer claimed that the disposition in favour of the defender was invalid in that her signature had been forged. She sought reduction of the disposition. There was a struggle by the pursuer to gain possession of the property which finally failed. As the defender had a registered title and had possession he could not be dispossessed of the property. Even if reduction of the disposition had been possible, it would have had no effect on the registered title.

Short's Tr v Chung (No 2) (1998): a trustee in sequestration claimed that the defender's property was part of the bankrupt estate and that the defender had acquired title by means of a gratuitous alienation made by the sequestrated party. The trustee sought a court order ordaining the defender to execute a disposition in favour of the trustee and thus gained possession of the property.

APPENDIX

STYLE DISPOSITION FOR A FIRST REGISTRATION

I, GEORGE SMITH residing at 17 Vine Place, Edinburgh, Heritable Proprietor of the subjects and others hereinafter disponed, IN CONSIDERATION of the price of ONE HUNDRED AND FORTY SIX THOUSAND POUNDS (£146,000) Sterling paid to me by JOHN JONES and Mrs. ELSIE MOOR or JONES, spouses, residing together at 19 Bank Street, Edinburgh, of which sum I hereby acknowledge the receipt, have sold and DO HEREBY DISPONE to the said John Jones and Mrs. Elsie Moor or Jones, and to their respective executors and assignees whomsoever heritably and irredeemably ALL and WHOLE that dwellinghouse and garden ground known as and forming number 17 Vine Place, Edinburgh in the County of Midlothian being the subjects particularly described in and disponed by and delineated and coloured pink on the plan annexed and executed as relative to the disposition by Edward Jenkins and Mrs. Eleanor Gosforth or Jenkins in my favour dated 23rd November and recorded in the Division of the General Register of Sasines applicable to the County of Midlothian on 5th December all in the year Nineteen hundred and eighty four; Together with (One) the whole fittings and fixtures therein and thereon, (Two) the whole rights, parts, privileges and pertinents thereof, and (Three) my whole right, title and interest, present and future, therein and thereto; But always with and under the burdens, conditions and others specified and contained in the said disposition in my favour; With entry and actual occupation on the 16th May Two thousand and four; And I grant warrandice; And I hereby declare that, until title is registered in the Land Register in pursuance of these presents, I hold the said subjects as trustee for behoof of the said John Jones and Mrs. Elsie Moor or Jones; : In witness whereof these presents are subscribed by me at Edinburgh on the 12th May Two thousand and four in the presence of Edith Westwood, solicitor, Royal Bank Chambers, 1 Bank Street, Edinburgh.

Note: that once a title is registered, the description will refer only to the postal address and the registered title number. There will therefore be no other verbal description or reference to any other deed. There will also be no reference to burdens as these will be noted in full on the title sheet.

INDEX